Research Methods in English Medium Instruction

In this special edited volume, the editors and invited English Medium Instruction (EMI) researchers, from different parts of the world, outline the latest EMI research methods. Providing academic instruction using English is rapidly spreading in many countries where English is a second or foreign language, and there is a growing interest in researching the effectiveness and effects of EMI across different educational levels. This volume includes chapters on everything from research into classroom interaction to teachers' and students' perceptions and motivations to language challenges and strategies and the pedagogical implications of translanguaging in EMI classrooms. These specific topics were chosen to reflect different approaches to researching EMI.

Each chapter focuses on a specific type of research methodology. It begins with an overview of the literature of the topic under discussion. Then an example study is provided to illustrate how this methodology can be used to investigate EMI. Each chapter identifies the process that the EMI researcher used to conduct their research and discusses key dilemmas they faced, focusing particularly on the methodological issues they encountered. By exploring these issues, this volume hopes to inform theory (or the lack thereof) underlying research into the phenomenon of EMI.

This volume is indispensable for EMI tutors, curriculum developers, policymakers, and teachers, as well as students at both undergraduate and postgraduate levels. It is particularly valuable for researchers from across the globe working in the fields of applied linguistics, language education, English for Academic Purposes (EAP), English Language Teaching (ELT), and Teaching English to Speakers of Other Languages (TESOL).

Jack K.H. Pun is an assistant professor in the Department of English at the City University of Hong Kong. He holds a doctorate in education from the University of Oxford, which explored the teaching and learning process in EMI science classrooms, with a special focus on classroom interactions, use of codeswitching, and teachers' and students' views of EMI. His research interests lie in EMI and health communication.

Samantha M. Curle is an assistant professor in the Department of Education at the University of Bath, UK. She completed her DPhil at the University of Oxford. She teaches subjects related to applied linguistics and is currently the director of the MRes Programme in Advanced Quantitative Research Methods. Her main research interest lies in factors affecting academic achievement in EMI. Her research has been published in journals such as *Language Teaching*, *Applied Linguistics Review*, *System*, and *International Journal of Bilingual Education and Bilingualism*.

Routledge Research in Higher Education

For more information about this series, please visit: *www.routledge.com/ Routledge-Research-in-Higher-Education/book-series/RRHE*

Research Methods in English Medium Instruction

Edited by Jack K.H. Pun and Samantha M. Curle

Routledge
Taylor & Francis Group

LONDON AND NEW YORK

First published 2022
by Routledge
2 Park Square, Milton Park, Abingdon, Oxon OX14 4RN

and by Routledge
605 Third Avenue, New York, NY 10158

Routledge is an imprint of the Taylor & Francis Group, an informa business

British Library Cataloguing-in-Publication Data
A catalogue record for this book is available from the British Library

Library of Congress Cataloging-in-Publication Data
A catalog record for this book has been requested

ISBN: 978-0-367-45755-6 (hbk)
ISBN: 978-1-032-10019-7 (pbk)
ISBN: 978-1-003-02511-5 (ebk)

DOI: 10.4324/9781003025115

Typeset in Times New Roman
by Apex CoVantage, LLC

This book is dedicated to Professor Ernesto Macaro

Contents

Contributors

Jack K.H. Pun is an assistant professor in the Department of English at the City University of Hong Kong. He holds a doctorate in education from the University of Oxford, which explored the teaching and learning process in EMI science classrooms, with a special focus on classroom interaction, use of codeswitching, and teachers' and students' views of EMI.

Samantha M. Curle is an assistant professor in the Department of Education at the University of Bath, UK. She completed her DPhil at the University of Oxford. She teaches subjects related to applied linguistics and is currently the director of the MRes Programme in Advanced Quantitative Research Methods. Her main research interest lies in factors affecting academic achievement in EMI. Her research has been published in journals such as *Language Teaching, Applied Linguistics Review, System,* and *International Journal of Bilingual Education and Bilingualism.*

Ali Derakhshan is an Associate Professor of Applied Linguistics at the English Language and Literature Department, Golestan University, Gorgan, Iran. He has published in both accredited international journals (*Applied Linguistics, Language Teaching Research, System, Journal of Pragmatics, Intercultural Pragmatics, Current Psychology,* etc.) and various local journals. His research interests are interlanguage pragmatics, teacher education, learner individual differences, EMI, and educational psychology in higher education.

Mairin Hennebry-Leung is a lecturer in languages and TESOL at the University of Tasmania. She has previously worked at the Universities of Oxford, Newcastle, and Edinburgh, having obtained her DPhil from the University of Oxford. Before embarking on a career in higher education, Mairin qualified as a modern languages teacher and worked in secondary school classrooms. Her research areas focus on language learning and teaching – primarily language learning motivation – language teacher education, and the relationship between language teaching and citizenship. Mairin's work has been published in journals such as *TESOL Quarterly*, *International Journal of Bilingual Education and Bilingualism*, *System*, *Language Learning Journal*, and the *Oxford Review of Education*, among others. She is Co-editor of the journal *System* as well as Co-editor of the Edinburgh University Press Textbooks in Applied Linguistics series. Mairin has delivered invited and keynote lectures, workshops, and seminars in diverse contexts including the United Kingdom, Ukraine, South Sudan, China, and Hong Kong.

Yuen Yi Lo is an associate professor in the Division of English Language Education of the Faculty of Education at the University of Hong Kong. She is also the deputy director of the master of education programme. She received her doctorate at the University of Oxford and has previously worked at the Hong Kong Education University. Her research interests include bilingual education, medium of instruction policy, codeswitching, and cross-curricular collaboration and assessment. Her research has been published in *Review of Educational Research*, *International Journal of Bilingual Education and Bilingualism*, *Language Teaching Research*, and *Language and Education*.

Gregg Dubow has over 15 years' experience in language training for specific purposes. As co-director of studies of the English Medium Instruction Project at the University of Freiburg, he has co-developed e-learning resources for teaching staff and a certification procedure to assess the linguistic and communicative competencies of teachers in English-taught programmes.

Susanne Gundermann holds a PhD in English Philology from the University of Freiburg. Her dissertation on EMI in higher education was awarded with the Erasmus Prize for the Liberal Arts and Sciences 2015. As co-director of studies of the English Medium Instruction Project at the University of Freiburg, she is responsible for providing training and feedback for lecturers and for developing quality criteria and assessment tools for EMI.

Louise Northover holds a master's degree in English language and linguistics. As co-director of studies of the English Medium Instruction Project at the University of Freiburg, she is responsible for offering individual and small-group training measures to develop and enhance communicative skills for teaching in English.

Reka R. Jablonkai's research interests include corpus-based discourse analysis, corpora in English language teaching and learning, teaching

ESP and EAP, and intercultural communication. She designed and compiled a one-million-word corpus for ESP pedagogic purposes for her doctoral research. She is grant holder of the Seedcorn research grant of the British Association of International and Comparative Education. She co-operates on research projects internationally and publishes in high-quality journals (e.g., *English for Specific Purposes*) and edited volumes. She works at the Language and Educational Practices Research Cluster at the University of Bath where she acts as the director of studies of the MA TESOL programme.

Mustafa Akincioglu worked at the University of Oxford in the Department of Education as a researcher from 2014 to 2018, where he was also involved in the design and delivery of EMI courses offered by the department. He continues his research on EMI as an associate researcher at the Oxford EMI Research Centre, while his research interests include critical discourse analysis, learner autonomy and learner motivation within EAP contexts, the EAP programme, and academic subject department collaboration development.

Yuwei Lin is a PhD candidate in the Department of Education at the University of Bath. Her research interests include EMI, students' willingness to communicate, and bilingual education.

Kevin W.H. Tai is a PhD candidate in applied linguistics in the UCL Centre for Applied Linguistics at the UCL Institute of Education, University College London. Kevin was recently invited to be Visiting Colleague in the Department of Second Language Studies at the University of Hawaii at Manoa. He completed his doctoral coursework in educational research at the University of Cambridge, where he was Hughes Hall Hong Kong Alumni Scholar. He holds an MSc degree in applied linguistics and second language acquisition from the University of Oxford. He graduated with his BA (honours) in English language and literature with first class honours at Newcastle University, UK. He was trained as a conversation analyst and he was awarded the Newcastle University Barbara Strang Best Performance Prize in Language and Linguistics for achieving the highest overall degree average in linguistics. Kevin is CELTA-qualified and his research interests include second language teaching and learning, sociocultural theories, classroom discourse, translanguaging practices in multilingual contexts, qualitative research methods, and second language teacher education. His research has appeared in international peer-reviewed journals such as *Classroom Discourse* and *Language and Education*.

1 Research methods for English Medium Instruction in action

Jack K.H. Pun and Samantha M. Curle

Abstract

This introductory chapter summarises the recent trends in EMI research and the kinds of methodologies used in such research. An outline of the rest of the chapters will also be provided. Each chapter represents different subfields of EMI studies – for example, exploring classroom interactions, teachers' and students' perceptions, translanguaging, and language challenges and strategies. The chapters also provide detailed accounts of how different EMI researchers conducted their research studies: what decision-making processes they went through in this research process, how they recruited participants and/or got access to data, and what research instruments they developed and/or adapted to yield the data they needed to answer their research questions.

Introduction

The provision of instruction of academic content in the English language is a rapidly growing practice in many countries where English is a second or foreign language. English language instruction has been implemented in a variety of forms in different places: for example, in Hong Kong, Malaysia, Singapore, Africa, Japan, and Korea, it is known as English Medium Instruction (EMI), whereas in Italy, Spain, Austria, and other European countries, it is called content and language integrated learning (CLIL). This volume focuses on EMI at both the secondary and tertiary education levels, at which research has shown that implementing EMI often has dual purposes: to improve students' academic content knowledge as well as their English language proficiency (see Dearden, 2015; Galloway, Kriukow, & Numajiri, 2017).

For this special edited volume, we have invited EMI researchers with close connections to the EMI Oxford research group, located in different parts of the world, to outline the latest research in EMI. According to the

DOI: 10.4324/9781003025115-1

latest systematic review of global EMI studies (Macaro, Curle, Pun, An, & Dearden, 2018), one of the growing topics within EMI studies is the implementation of EMI instruction. Within this area of research interest, the volume covers classroom interaction, perceptions of EMI among teachers and students, and language-related challenges and associated coping strategies. There is also growing research interest in the field of translanguaging in EMI classrooms (see Curle, Jablonkai, Mittelmeier, Sahan, & Veitch, 2020). We therefore include a chapter dedicated to this topic, for which the author was invited to discuss the pedagogical implications of translanguaging in EMI classrooms. These specific topics were chosen to reflect the variety of research methodologies being applied to EMI studies and the range of phenomena that are currently receiving research attention in the field.

Each chapter is focused on a specific type of research methodology, and many provide research instruments for the use of future researchers. Before reporting on its respective case study, each chapter begins with an overview of the relevant literature and the research methods that were applied. The volume thereby differs from the majority of EMI-related books by presenting case studies addressing central themes in EMI research alongside explanations of the research methods and instruments used to generate the findings. The chapters identify the processes that were followed by EMI researchers as they conducted their research, the key dilemmas they faced, and the methodological issues they encountered. Exploring these issues can inform theories underlying research into EMI and help to develop theory where it is lacking. This volume will be an indispensable resource for EMI tutors, education curriculum officers, and researchers, as well as education policymakers, secondary and tertiary education researchers, and undergraduate and postgraduate students in the fields of applied linguistics, language education, English for specific purposes, ELT, and TESOL.

The English language is taught at the elementary and secondary levels in many countries in which English is not the primary language. Until recently, this language education was mostly focused on establishing or improving students' English communication skills, with English having been rarely used for content learning purposes. However, there have been major changes in the use of English in education in non-English-speaking countries over the last two decades, with EMI becoming a global phenomenon in secondary and higher education. In addition to teaching students to communicate in English, many institutions now teach certain subjects, such as science and history, in English. At last count, almost 8,000 courses were being taught in English at universities in non-English-speaking countries. The key sites for this change are higher education institutions, especially in Asia, where extensive research into EMI teaching is conducted (Tsou & Kao, 2017). For example, all universities in

Hong Kong have adopted EMI as a primary teaching mode (Poon & Lau, 2016). With a growing global interest in EMI studies and the implementation of EMI in both universities and secondary schools, a methodological exploration is now warranted.

Three main reasons have been given for the aforementioned rapid growth in the implementation of EMI: (1) the rise of English as a global lingua franca, (2) the expansion of English within the Asia-Pacific region in particular, and (3) the growth of internationalisation as a feature of government education policies (Fenton-Smith, Humphreys, & Walkinshaw, 2017). In the following chapters, the research methods and instruments used to generate findings are discussed in relation to various case studies. The book then outlines the processes that EMI researchers have followed in their research and some of the major challenges they have encountered, particularly in relation to methodological issues.

1.1 Research methods in EMI studies

Studies of EMI at the secondary and tertiary levels have had slightly different focuses and have thus called for a variety of methods. Most research into EMI at the secondary school level has involved comparisons between immersion and non-immersion students on their performance in English and L1, content learning, and cognitive development. Most of these studies have used tests to measure the performance of different groups of students. Another major topic has been the feedback from teachers, students, and parents regarding their experiences with EMI. These studies have typically used questionnaires and interviews for data collection. Questionnaires have also been widely used in studies exploring children's readiness for EMI education and the impact of EMI on students' motivation to learn English. Other studies have used classroom observations to collect data to explore a range of topics relating to EMI such as (1) how EMI classrooms provide opportunities for students to learn the English language alongside the content, (2) the discursive practices in EMI classrooms, (3) codeswitching behaviours, (4) the strategic use of multimedia, and (5) comparing EMI and English as a Foreign Language (EFL) classes. Another set of studies has used genre analysis to explore the text genres in EMI textbooks, the social impact of EMI, and the link between EMI policies and children's sociocultural ecology.

At the tertiary level, most studies exploring the effects of EMI on student achievement in English language and content have compared EMI and non-EMI classrooms. These studies have used tests to measure students' receptive and productive vocabularies, reading comprehension, and actual L1 and L2 language use. Several studies have also explored the attitudes of teachers and students towards EMI and the development of teaching approaches for combining instruction in content and language. Data collection methods used in these studies have included semi-structured interviews, questionnaires, classroom observations, discourse analysis of lesson transcripts, student writing and learning materials, and some document analysis.

More generally, the topics discussed in studies of EMI can be categorised into six major areas, with each having its own research methodology. The first area involves comparisons between EMI and non-EMI students in their English and L1 performances, content learning, and cognitive development. Research into language policy provides empirical evidence of the correlations between the use of different mediums of instruction (e.g., Chinese or English) and students' academic achievements. Academic achievements are measured by students' school examination results in their language subjects (e.g., EFL and Chinese) and content subjects (e.g., mathematics, science). In Hong Kong, for example, Yip and Tsang (2007) conducted a longitudinal study of a sample of 12,000 students to investigate the effects on student achievement of the compulsory mother-tongue policy introduced in 1998 on student science learning during the first two years of junior secondary school (grades 7 and 8) in EMI and Chinese Medium Instruction (CMI) groups. Drawing on 100 EMI and CMI schools, they recruited grade 7 students with equal academic achievements prior to their admission to secondary school and measured their achievements in science subjects at grades 7, 8, and 9. EMI and CMI groups were compared using science achievement tests, questionnaires about their self-concept in science, and classroom observations of science lessons. The results showed that EMI junior secondary school students had higher science achievement scores than all but the most able CMI students at the same level, but EMI students generally held a lower self-concept than CMI students. Yip and Tsang (2007) concluded that when using L2, EMI students experience greater difficulties in trying to understand abstract concepts, making distinctions between scientific terms and applying concepts in different situations. From their observations of EMI classrooms, they further concluded that EMI negatively affected the quality of science learning due to limited English proficiency on the part of students and inadequate repertoires of instructional strategies on the part of teachers.

The second area is exploring the feedback from teachers, students, and parents regarding their experiences with EMI. For example, Chan (2014) explored the views of the principal, teachers, and students in content-subject classrooms during the implementation in Hong Kong of the fine-tuning language policy in 2010. Three methods were used in Chan's (2014) study: (1) focus groups and semi-structured individual interviews with students and school staff members, (2) an open-ended questionnaire administered to a large student sample, and (3) analysis of non-participant and unstructured observations to supplement the qualitative data. The study showed that the increase in the amount of EMI teaching presented many language-related challenges to students and generated pedagogical and practical issues in content-subject classrooms. Two of the findings were that students with lower English proficiency faced major difficulties in learning content in EMI subjects, and that teachers would sometimes overemphasise memorisation of material and neglect to promote higher-order thinking skills. Chan (2014) thus argued that the increased amount of EMI instruction was benefiting more capable students at the cost of sacrificing the interests and learning needs of less capable students because time constraints prevented the realisation of a dual focus on language and content. Under the fine-tuning policy, Chan (2014) concluded that less capable students might be equally or even further disadvantaged compared to students in CMI schools who were not receiving a bilingual education but could obtain more content knowledge.

The third area is exploring through classroom observation how EMI classrooms provide opportunities for students to learn English. Research into classroom interactions in the context of EMI has been mainly focused on teacher-student interactions and the EMI teaching practices of individual science teachers (Chan, 2013, 2014; Lin, 2006; Lo & Macaro, 2012; Lo, 2014; Wannagat, 2007; Yip, Coyle, & Tsang, 2007). These studies take an ethnographic approach, using observations and interviews together with discourse analysis to identify patterns of interactions between teachers and their students. For example, Lo and Macaro (2012) used classroom observations to compare classroom interactions between EMI and MOI-switching secondary schools (those that had moved from adopting CMI to allowing EMI) in Hong Kong. They compared the quality of L2 language learning in humanities and science classrooms by the number of turns that students took at talking, the length of these turns, and the Initiation-Response-Feedback (IRF) patterns (Sinclair & Coulthard, 1975), while also identifying types of form-focused exchanges by paying attention to specific grammatical rules and lexical items (Costa, 2012). The observation of 22 lessons at grades 9 and 10 showed that science lessons were teacher-centred, and the analysis of IRF sequences showed a significantly lower proportion of student talk characterised by frequent short turns. Teachers also paid less attention to form-focused instruction in L2. Both the register of science and the availability of other semiotic resources for teaching science were found to have reduced the L2 language learning opportunities that would otherwise arise from engaging students in class discussions and interactions with their teacher. Lo and Macaro's (2012) study revealed a dilemma encountered by teachers in MOI-switching schools: although making use of L1 might slow the process of learning English, the full use of EMI might inhibit the peda-gogical processes that support deeper learning.

The fourth area is examining the effects of EMI experiences on students' motivation to learn English. Researchers in this area hold that the nature of the interactions between MOI and language learning motivation (LLM) is important due to the significance of LLM for attaining language skills (Hennebry & Gao, 2018; Jiang, Zhang, & May, 2019). For example, Hennebry and Gao (2018) examined interactions between English LLM and different MOI settings. Purposive, stratified sampling was used to recruit 3,854 Hong Kong secondary school students from four EMI, five mixed-medium instruction (MMI), and two CMI schools. Questionnaires are recommended for examining motivation in the field of psychology in general and specifically in studies of LLM (see Bernaus & Gardner, 2008; Chen, Warden, & Chang, 2005; Gardner & Tremblay, 1994). Accordingly, Hennebry and Gao (2018) administered a questionnaire comprising scales for measuring a range of English LLM constructs. It was found that EMI students showed higher motivations for learning English than CMI and MMI students, thus suggesting that EMI classrooms provide motivation to learn English. Although the results indicated similar motivational profiles across the three MOIs, EMI students scored highest on the required orientation and the instrumental promotion orientation. This finding supports the idea that LLM is responsive to contextual features, as these orientations were the highest scales across the MOI settings.

The fifth major area is the genre analysis of text genres in EMI text-books. Studies in this area have mainly focused on the language features of these texts, which are written in English and present content, not language instruction. On the basis that EMI textbooks are the primary linguistic resources for ESL students to learn the content and language, or jargon, of a subject, studies have investigated how the subject knowledge is presented in textbooks and have explored the most common types of texts that students would encounter and from which they would learn (see Maxwell-Reid & Lau, 2016; Llinares, Morton, & Whittaker, 2012; Fang, 2005). For example, Pun (2019) examined certain language features that science students would encounter in EMI chemistry textbooks. Three chemistry textbooks commonly used in Hong Kong secondary EMI classrooms were selected and analysed, with a functional linguistic approach adopted to identify the nature of the explanatory texts. For this purpose, an experienced senior science teacher was recruited from a local school as a co-researcher. The co-researcher was trained to code sample texts based on Veel's (1997) taxonomy, and the coding was cross-checked for consistency with Pun's analysis. It was found that the most common text type in the three text-books was explanation, of which five subtypes were identified: from most to least common, they are causal, factorial, sequential, consequential, and theoretical explanations. The features and distributions of these subtypes were examined to reveal the kinds of language mostly encountered by EMI chemistry students. The results indicate that explanatory texts played a primary linguistic role in the facilitation of EMI students learning the language of science. This research area promises to help future pedagogists make EMI chemistry, or even broader science, textbooks more suitable for and more accessible to students learning in a second language. The findings from studies in this area can also help educators effectively balance content and language learning.

The sixth major research area in EMI studies is policy analysis. Studies within this area have focused on the development of and changes in language policies in education. The main factors of policymaking are political, historical, economic, and educational, as shown in studies of Hong Kong's fine-tuning MOI policy implemented in 2010 (Poon, Lau, & Chu, 2013; Poon, 2010). Poon's (2010) monograph, for example, views the MOI situation in Hong Kong from a historical perspective. The multicultural city of Hong Kong is characterised by (1) official languages, (2) main minority languages, and (3) actual language use, which involves a wide range of code-mixing, codeswitching, and bilingualism. The main methods used in this study were a literature review and document analysis. From an analysis of data taken from government censuses, which include the population, GDP, and proportions of various spoken languages in daily life, it was concluded that Hong Kong's language community started with two separate monolingual groups: local people who spoke Cantonese and/or other Chinese dialects (Luke & Richards, 1982) and British colonists who spoke British English. From this foundation, language spread and language shifts occurred in Hong Kong due to political, economic, and social changes: the monolingual group of Cantonese speakers became trilingual (speaking Cantonese, English, and Mandarin), the group of native British English speakers expanded to include wider varieties of English, and a large group of bilingual/trilingual speakers emerged who could speak English, Cantonese, and a South Asian language (Poon, 2010). This made the MOI in local schools a controversial issue. Another study in this area was that of Evans (2013), who studied the promotion of biliteracy and trilingualism in Hong Kong education since the 1997 handover. Although the primary languages used in Hong Kong at this time were Cantonese and English, increasing political and economic integration with China going back to the early 1980s made the promotion of Mandarin (or Putonghua) in the education system both desirable and inevitable (Evans, 2013). In his study, Evans (2013) carried out a literature review and analysed documents and data, reviewing a large quantity of research on various topics relating to MOI policy such as implementation, teaching and learning processes, and learning outcomes. The results indicate the advantages of mother-tongue (in this case, Cantonese) teaching and the problems associated with L2-medium instruction (in this case, in English or Putonghua). It was concluded that the promotion of biliteracy and trilingualism raised critical questions about the role of research in language policymaking.

1.2   A detailed synopsis, including chapter summaries

1.2.1   Proposed structure for each chapter

In putting together this volume, we adopted the approach of McKinley and Rose (2016). Each chapter has a similar structure: (1) project overview and context, including information about the fundamental focus of the research project, the method(s) used, and the reasons for using those specific method(s), (2) research planning, indicating the decisions made while setting up the project, (3) research design, including an explanation of the study design suitable for student readers that gives consideration to any fundamental decisions that were made, (4) details on methods (data collection, analysis and reporting), including the description and evaluation of the execution of the chosen research method(s), the challenges that emerged, and the resolution of these challenges, (5) practical lessons learned, the most important section of a research methods case study, which includes in-depth reflections on the specific method(s) used and important lessons learnt during the implementation, and (6) a concluding summary, which includes a round-up of the issues discussed in the case study. This final section is a discussion not merely of the conclusions drawn from the findings but also of the conclusions drawn from methodological reflections. The focus is on the method(s) used for the research area and suggestions of any more suitable method(s) for future research within the same area. Upholding this structure in each chapter increases the coherence of the book.

The first chapter is an introduction summarising recent trends in EMI research and the methods used for addressing particular topics. This introduction also summarises the chapters as representing different subfields of EMI studies (e.g., classroom interactions, perceptions of teachers and students, translanguaging, language challenges, and learners' strategies) and provides detailed accounts of how the researchers conducted their studies, what decisions were made in this research process, how they recruited participants or gained access to data, and what research instruments they developed, adopted, or adapted to gather the data they needed to answer their research questions.

In Chapter 2, Pun reports on a study in Hong Kong that explored the teaching and learning process in EMI science classrooms (physics, chemistry, and biology) in eight secondary schools. His study drew on 34 hours of video-recorded classroom observations involving 19 teachers and 545 grade 10 and 11 students to investigate the patterns of classroom interactions (e.g., turn-taking, ratio of talk, language choices, and question types) in both full EMI and MOI-switching schools. Pun also discusses the method of observational data collection, presenting the observation scheme used in the study and providing insights into the challenges involved in collecting, processing, and analysing this type of data. Pun's research provides an evidence-based and detailed analysis of authentic classroom interactions that is aimed at improving the quality of instructional practices in EMI classrooms worldwide.

In Chapter 3, Curle and Derakhshan present a critical analysis of the use of questionnaires in EMI research. EMI researchers have made extensive use of questionnaires, but most have fallen short in applying questionnaire design theory to their questionnaire development and implementation. Curle and Derakhshan claim that this oversight can directly and negatively affect the accuracy of data obtained in this fashion. As a review study, this chapter describes the use of questionnaires in EMI research with a specific focus on the challenges and risks involved in design and implementation. Stepwise suggestions to enhance the robustness of the psychometric properties of the scales used in these questionnaires are also presented in the chapter.

Hennebry-Leung adopts an agentive view of the learner in Chapter 4, which explores the interplay between contextual factors and LLM in EMI classrooms in Hong Kong, with a focus on what this relationship means for how motivation is conceptualised and studied. Specifically, Hennebry-Leung examines the tools that have been used most often in studies of LLM in EMI contexts and critically discusses their suitability for capturing the complex interplay between contextual factors and learner motivation, particularly within an EMI context.

In the fifth chapter, Lo first reviews some important research questions related to assessment in EMI. She then introduces a framework for analysing the cognitive and linguistic demands of assessment questions that have been adopted in a number of recent research studies on EMI assessment in Hong Kong. Using such a framework for analysing assessment questions in EMI helps not only to reveal current practices of EMI assessment but also to identify the features of valid assessment design and effective pedagogy in EMI.

In Chapter 6, Dubow, Gundermann, and Northover present EMI-specific criteria to expand on perceived gaps in quality assurance measures. Although students can be required to prove their language competencies (usually at the C1 level based on the *Common European Framework of Reference for Languages* [CEFR]) for admittance into an EMI programme, many universities have assumed that teachers possess the necessary language skills to teach in an EMI programme. Only a few systematic measures have been taken to certify the speaking proficiency of teachers in EMI programmes in Europe; these measures assessed the oral skills of teachers in EMI programmes in test settings but without the presence of students as the most vital stakeholders. Consequently, there was no assessment of the additional communicative competencies for teaching a multilingual and multicultural group of students. Research has shown, however, that teacher competencies such as dialogical teaching, intercultural transparency, and accommodation strategies for English as a lingua franca are regularly cited by students as being helpful in facilitating their content learning in EMI settings. This chapter outlines these EMI-specific criteria, gives insights into their application based on quantitative and qualitative data from the authors' assessment practices, and suggests some implications for EMI practitioners.

In Chapter 7, Jablonkai reviews studies of the corpora of classroom discourse and academic disciplinary discourse in EMI contexts. Although corpus linguistic methods are widely used to analyse educational and professional discourse, this chapter reviews the surprisingly few studies applying this approach in EMI contexts. These studies, focusing on English used as a lingua franca in the Finnish higher education context, have investigated communicative strategies and described the core features of this language use. Rather than identifying features that emerge from the corpus by applying a corpus-driven approach (Biber & Barbieri, 2007; Tognini-Bonelli, 2001), corpus-based studies often use corpus linguistic methods in combination with qualitative methods, such as conversational analysis (Jawhar, 2012) and pragmatic frameworks (Björkman, 2011), or investigate the patterns of use of pre-selected lexical items (Dafouz, Núñez, & Sancho, 2007; Molino, 2018) in their respective corpora. In addressing these limitations and how they might be mitigated in an EMI linguistic context, Jablonkai demonstrates how the potential of corpora and corpus linguistic methods might be realised in EMI research.

In Chapter 8, Akincioglu and Li report on an experiment in language and content learning collaboration conducted in Turkey. English language teachers from English language preparatory programmes of EMI universities and EMI teachers from EMI academic subject departments were given a research instrument, the Collaborative Lesson Planning Tool, and guidelines for how the collaboration might proceed. After the collaboration, reflective interviews were conducted to shed light on the more and less successful aspects of the experiment. In this chapter, Akincioglu and Li elaborate on and critically discuss the collaboration tool based on how much time the collaboration took, how the motivation of lecturers influenced the level of collaboration, and how collaboration can best be tailored to the needs of language teachers and EMI lecturers.

In Chapter 9, Tai explores the possibility of combining conversation analysis (CA) with an ethnographic approach to better understand how translanguaging practices are realised in EMI classrooms, and how translanguaging can facilitate content and language learning in an EMI context. Most translanguaging research in EMI and CLIL classrooms has used functional discourse analysis (e.g., Duarte, 2019; Poza, 2018; Lin & Lo, 2017) and ethnographic techniques (e.g., Mazak & Herbas-Donoso, 2015; Lin & He, 2017) to explore how teachers and bilingual learners communicate and create meaning through translanguaging. Very few studies (e.g., Moore, 2014; Lin & Wu, 2015; Jakonen, Szabó, & Laihonen, 2018) have used CA to conduct a fine-grained analysis of classroom talk to detail the functions that translanguaging serves in EMI classrooms. To explore the possibility of combining these methods, Tai draws on the preliminary analysis of his PhD pilot study, which was carried out at a Hong Kong EMI secondary mathematics classroom. This chapter argues that CA can go beyond revealing the functions of translanguaging and enable researchers to discover the complex multilingual and multimodal resources used by translanguaging interactants to co-construct meanings in EMI classroom interactions. In addition, taking an ethnographic approach can help researchers understand how the wider sociocultural contexts and the identities of the participants play roles in translanguaging practices.

1.3 A description of the target market

This edited volume will provide up-to-date insights into appropriate research methods for studying EMI in various contexts across the globe. The book will be highly relevant to scholars in the field of educational linguistics, particularly those with research interests in English language teaching, content-based instruction, content and language integrated learning, and EMI. It will also be valuable for teachers and students, the key EMI stakeholders. The book will serve as a reference for EMI practitioners seeking ideas for action research to enhance teaching and learning. For example, administering the attitudes towards EMI research instrument to their students might provide lecturers with insights into why their students have chosen an EMI course. Lecturers could then adapt their teaching to meet these expectations. Furthermore, the template research instruments and their annotations will be particularly valuable to EMI researchers and instructors doing EMI professional development courses, as they showcase ways of applying different methods and techniques to EMI research. Undergraduate or postgraduate students conducting research in the field will also find this volume to be of practical use. Finally, education policymakers can gain insights from the book into how to conduct research on the effectiveness of EMI policies. The methodological guidelines provided within will be useful when commissioning research into policy implementation.

References

Bernaus, M., & Gardner, R. C. (2008). Teacher motivation strategies, student perceptions, student motivation, and English achievement. *The Modern Language Journal, 92*(3), 387–401.

Biber, D., & Barbieri, F. (2007). Lexical bundles in university spoken and written registers. *English for Specific Purposes, 26*(3), 263–286.

Björkman, B. (2011). Pragmatic strategies in English as an academic lingua franca: Ways of achieving communicative effectiveness?. *Journal of Pragmatics, 43*(4), 950–964.

Chan, J. Y. H. (2013). A week in the life of a 'finely tuned' secondary school in Hong Kong. *Journal of Multilingual and Multicultural Development, 34*(5), 411–430.

Chan, J. Y. H. (2014). Fine-tuning language policy in Hong Kong education: Stakeholders' perceptions, practices and challenges. *Language and Education, 28*(5), 459–476.

Chen, J. F., Warden, C. A., & Chang, H. T. (2005). Motivators that do not motivate: The case of Chinese EFL learners and the influence of culture on motivation. *TESOL Quarterly, 39*(4), 609–633.

Costa, F. (2012). Focus on form in ICLHE lectures in Italy: Evidence from English-medium science lectures by native speakers of Italian. *AILA Review, 25*(1), 30–47.

Curle, S., Jablonkai, R., Mittelmeier, J., Sahan, K., & Veitch, A. (2020). English medium part 1: Literature review. In N. Galloway (Ed.), English in higher education (Report No. 978-0-86355-977-8). British Council. Retrieved from www. teachingenglish.org.uk/sites/teacheng/files/L020_English_HE_lit_review_ FINAL.pdf

Dafouz, E., Núñez, B., & Sancho, C. (2007). Analysing stance in a CLIL university context: Non-native speaker use of personal pronouns and modal verbs. *International Journal of Bilingual Education and Bilingualism, 10*(5), 647–662.

Dearden, J. (2015). *English as a medium of instruction – A growing global phenomenon*. British Council. Retrieved from www.britishcouncil.es/sites/default/files/ british_council_english_as_a_medium_of_instruction.pdf.

Duarte, J. (2019). Translanguaging in mainstream education: A sociocultural approach. *International Journal of Bilingual Education and Bilingualism, 22*(2), 150–164.

Evans, S. (2013). The long march to biliteracy and trilingualism: Language policy in Hong Kong education since the handover. *Annual Review of Applied Linguistics, 33*, 302–324.

Fang, Z. (2005). Scientific literacy: A systemic functional linguistics perspective. *Science Education, 89*, 335–347.

Fenton-Smith, B., Humphreys, P., & Walkinshaw, I. (2017). *English medium instruction in higher education in Asia-Pacific* (Multilingual Education, 21). Cham: Springer.

Galloway, N., Kriukow, J., & Numajiri, T. (2017). *Internationalisation, higher education and the growing demand for English: An investigation into the English medium of instruction (EMI) movement in China and Japan.* British Council Report.

Gardner, R. C., & Tremblay, P. F. (1994). On motivation, research agendas, and theoretical frameworks 1. *The Modern Language Journal, 78*(3), 359–368.

Hennebry, M., & Gao, X. (2018). Interactions between medium of instruction and language learning motivation. *International Journal of Bilingual Education and Bilingualism*, 1–14.

Jakonen, T., Szabó, T. P., & Laihonen, P. (2018). Translanguaging as playful subversion of a monolingual norm in the classroom. In *Translanguaging as everyday practice* (pp. 31–48). Cham: Springer.

Jawhar, S. (2012). *Conceptualising CLIL in a Saudi context: A corpus linguistic and conversation analytic perspective* (Doctoral dissertation). Newcastle University, Newcastle upon Tyne, UK. Retrieved from https://theses.ncl.ac.uk/dspace/bitstream/10443/1849/1/Jawhar12.pdf.

Jiang, L., Zhang, L. J., & May, S. (2019). Implementing English-medium instruction (EMI) in China: Teachers' practices and perceptions, and students' learning motivation and needs. *International Journal of Bilingual Education and Bilingualism, 22*(2), 107–119.

Lin, A. M. Y. (2006). Beyond linguistic purism in language-in-education policy and practice: Exploring bilingual pedagogies in a Hong Kong science classroom. *Language and Education, 20*(4), 287–305.

Lin, A. M. Y., & He, P. (2017). Translanguaging as dynamic activity flows in CLIL classrooms. *Journal of Language, Identity & Education, 16*(4), 228–244.

Lin, A. M. Y., & Lo, Y. Y. (2017). Trans/languaging and the triadic dialogue in content and language integrated learning (CLIL) classrooms. *Language and Education, 31*, 26–45.

Lin, A. M. Y., & Wu, Y. (2015). 'May I speak Cantonese?' – Co-constructing a scientific proof in an EFL junior secondary science classroom. *International Journal of Bilingual Education and Bilingualism, 18*, 289–305.

Llinares, A., Morton, T., & Whittaker, R. (2012). *The roles of language in CLIL.* Cambridge: Cambridge University Press.

Lo, Y. Y. (2014). L2 learning opportunities in different academic subjects in content-based instruction-evidence in favour of 'conventional wisdom'. *Language and Education, 28*(2), 141–160.

Lo, Y. Y., & Macaro, E. (2012). The medium of instruction and classroom interaction: Evidence from Hong Kong secondary schools. *International Journal of Bilingual Education and Bilingualism, 15*(1), 29–52.

Luke, K. K., & Richards, J. C. (1982). English in Hong Kong: Functions and status. *English World Wide*, *3*(1), 47–64.

Macaro, E., Curle, S., Pun, J., An, J., & Dearden, J. (2018). A systematic review of English medium instruction in higher education. *Language Teaching*, *51*(1).

Maxwell-Reid, C., & Lau, K. C. (2016). Genre and technicality in analogical explanations: Hong Kong's English language textbooks for junior secondary science. *Journal of English for Academic Purposes*, *23*, 31–46.

Mazak, C., & Herbas-Donoso, C. (2015). Translanguaging practices at a bilingual university: A case study of a science classroom. *International Journal of Bilingual Education and Bilingualism*, *18*, 698–714.

McKinley, J., & Rose, H. (Eds.). (2016). *Doing research in applied linguistics: Realities, dilemmas, and solutions*. New York: Taylor & Francis.

Molino, A. (2018). 'What I'm speaking is almost English. . .': A corpus-based study of metadiscourse in English-medium lectures at an Italian university. *Educational Sciences: Theory & Practice*, *18*(4), 935–956.

Moore, E. (2014). Constructing content and language knowledge in plurilingual student teamwork: Situated and longitudinal perspectives. *International Journal of Bilingual Education and Bilingualism*, *17*, 586–609.

Poon, A. Y. K. (2010). Language use, and language policy and planning in Hong Kong. *Current Issues in Language Planning*, *11*(1), 1–66.

Poon, A. Y. K., & Lau, C. M. Y. (2016). Fine-tuning medium-of-instruction policy in Hong Kong: Acquisition of language and content-based subject knowledge. *Journal of Pan-Pacific Association of Applied Linguistics*, *20*(1), 135–155.

Poon, A. Y. K., Lau, C. M. Y., & Chu, D. H. (2013). Impact of the fine-tuning medium-of-instruction policy on learning: Some preliminary findings. *Literacy Information and Computer Education Journal*, *4*(1), 946–954.

Poza, L. E. (2018). The language of *ciencia*: Translanguaging and learning in a bilingual science classroom. *International Journal of Bilingual Education and Bilingualism*, *21*(1), 1–19.

Pun, J. K. (2019). Salient language features in explanation texts that students encounter in secondary school chemistry textbooks. *Journal of English for Academic Purposes*, *42*, 100781.

Sinclair, J. M., & Coulthard, M. (1975). *Towards an analysis of discourse: The English used by teachers and pupils*. Oxford: Oxford University Press.

Tognini-Bonelli, E. (2001). *Corpus linguistics at work*. Amsterdam: John Benjamins.

Tsou, W., & Kao, S. (2017). *English as a medium of instruction in higher education: Implementations and classroom practices in Taiwan* (English Language Education, 8). Singapore: Springer Singapore.

Veel, R. (1997). Learning how to mean – scientifically speaking: Apprenticeship into scientific discourse in the secondary school. *Genre and Institutions: Social Processes in the Workplace and School*, *161*, 195.

Wannagat, U. (2007). Learning through L2 – Content and language integrated learning (CLIL) and English as medium of instruction (EMI). *International Journal of Bilingual Education and Bilingualism, 10*(5), 663–682.

Yip, D. Y., Coyle, D., & Tsang, W. K. (2007). Evaluation of the effects of the medium of instruction on science learning of Hong Kong secondary students: Instructional activities in science lessons. *Education Journal, 35*(2), 77–107.

Yip, D. Y., & Tsang, W. K. (2007). Evaluation of the effects of the medium of instruction on science learning of Hong Kong secondary students: Students' self-concept in science. *International Journal of Science and Mathematics Education, 5*(3), 393–413.

2 Research conducted on classroom interaction in the English Medium Instruction context

Jack K.H. Pun

Abstract

Teaching science through English is a growing phenomenon around the world. In this chapter, I start off by providing an overview of the challenges that teachers and students face when learning science through English in various cultural contexts. I then move on to report a study in Hong Kong which explores the teaching and learning process in EMI science classrooms (physics, chemistry, biology) from eight secondary schools. Drawing on 34 hours of video-recorded classroom observations of 19 teachers and 545 students, I explore the patterns of classroom interactions (turn-taking, ratio of talk, language choices, question types) in traditional (or early-full) EMI versus MOI-switching (or late-partial) schools (switching from L1 Cantonese to L2 English), between grades 10 and 11. I discuss the method of observational data collection; challenges collecting, processing, and analysing this type of data. I then provide the observation scheme used in this study. By providing an evidence-based, detailed analysis of authentic classroom interactions, this research hopefully sheds light on ways for improving the quality of instructional practices in different EMI classrooms worldwide.

2.1 Overview and context

English – one of the most spoken languages – has not only been taught around the world but also used to teach (Galloway, Kriukow, & Numajiri, 2017). English Medium Instruction (EMI) is a global trend in higher education institutions, especially in a growing number of non-English-speaking countries worldwide, in a globalisation and marketisation context (Coleman, 2006; Macaro, 2018). There are several reasons for adopting EMI in education, most significantly in higher education. The reasons include academic internationalisation, teaching and research materials available, and graduate employability (Macaro, Curle, Pun, An, & Dearden, 2018). However, previous studies have

DOI: 10.4324/9781003025115-2

shown that EMI instruction might be challenging for some content-subject teachers as well as students. Students with lower English proficiencies sometimes struggle to learn subject content with their second language (Lin, 2012). According to Lo and Lo (2014), the academic and cognitive development of students, who learn through an unfamiliar second language, might be slower than that of the others who learn with their first language.

2.1.1 Why researchers are interested in exploring classroom interactions as a method

Classroom talk is an essential part of classrooms and evidence shows that how teachers talk guides learners in their understanding of the content. McDonough and McDonough (1997) illustrated classroom observation as a research method for directly observing the teaching in real time in order to gain an understanding of the teaching practices. Creswell (2003) believed that observation allows one to analyse different aspects of the classroom, allowing first-hand experience and access to information as it unfolds. Previous research had shown that classroom discourse is an essential component to students' construction and acquisition of knowledge mediated through teachers' pedagogical scaffolding. Student-teacher interaction constitutes a core component of classroom discourse. Hence, allowing students to freely express their lack of comprehension of the learning content and elicit teacher feedback about the subject matter. Researchers in the field of science education have shown that skilful questioning by teachers can promote meaningful learning.

The concept of scaffolding and Vygotsky's (1997) social constructive theory of learning are closely connected. In Vygotsky's viewpoint, learning takes place in social interaction. This includes collaborating with others and interacting with them. When used in social activities, language can serve as a mediating tool in all forms of higher-order mental processing such as logical problem-solving, planning, evaluating, and learning (Swain & Lapkin, 2000). Ho, Wong, and Rappa (2019) examined how teachers provided scaffolding through purposeful classroom discourse (Lemke, 1990) with the use of talk moves (Chapin & Anderson, 2013). For instance, the students generated concept sketches as an initial step of learning from which other communication modes were created. The visual representation on its own was insufficient in generating meaning. The study acknowledges the teacher's role in the classroom discourse in guiding students' thought processes and facilitating meaning-making. The main focus was to examine teacher-facilitated classroom discussions. By observing classroom interactions, researchers can learn more about the benefits and shortcomings of EMI's reality. This chapter will briefly report the classroom interaction studies conducted in the EMI context and summarise a few key analytical frameworks for conducting classroom interaction analysis.

2.1.2 Research planning and design

To synthesise the findings from previous studies on EMI classroom interactions, three databases – ERIC, SCOPUS, and PSYINFO – were included to search and identify relevant articles between 2010 and 2020. Keywords such as "classroom", "interaction", and "English Medium Instruction" were used for locating related articles online. These databases initially identified around 1,000 studies after the title and abstract screening. Full articles were retrieved, and in-depth data extraction was performed if the abstracts were considered potentially relevant. The objectives, research design, participant characteristics, study design, method(s) and key findings were recorded in template form, categorised, and appraised for quality. In the final review, to explore EMI interactions in classrooms, 18 articles were included. Emerging from Hong Kong, China, Japan, and South Africa, these studies investigated the role of classroom interactions and the pedagogical functions of using L1 and L2.

Table 2.1 shows the main characteristics of the 18 included studies, with a summary of the main findings. These findings were extracted and categorised into three themes:

1   amount and pedagogical functions of classroom interactions
2   codeswitching and translanguaging practices
3   individual teaching strategies

Research on classroom interactions in EMI primarily focuses on the actual amount and pedagogical functions of teacher and student talk in observed classroom interactions (Lo & Macaro, 2012; Marsh, Hau, & Kong, 2000; Pun & Macaro, 2019; Wannagat, 2007; Yip, Coyle, & Tsang, 2007). The second strand of research explores individual teaching practices of content-subject teachers in the context of EMI classrooms (Chan, 2013, 2014; Lin, 2006; Probyn, 2009). The third strand of research looks at how teachers and students use codeswitching or translanguaging in mediating content-subject concepts for effective classroom interactions.

2.2 Amount and pedagogical functions of classroom interactions

Research on classroom interactions in the context of EMI principally focuses on teacher-student interactions and the teaching practices of

Table 2.1 The characteristics of the studies

[*Please go online via URL link: https://docs.google.com/document/d/17yO_hqG89RPhfiL9kBePIlUxU2aBRKcm6cdZDI-0l-A/edit?usp=sharing]

individual science teachers in the context of EMI classrooms (Chan, 2013, 2014; Lin, 2006; Lo & Macaro, 2012; Lo, 2014; Wannagat, 2007; Yip et al., 2007). These studies employ an ethnographic approach (observations and interviews), together with discourse analysis, and identify patterns of interactions between the teacher and students. These studies describe different types of talk and pedagogies for delivering scientific content through English or code-mixing between Cantonese and English.

Lo and Macaro (2012) explored the interaction between EMI and MOI-switching secondary schools using classroom observation. They examined the quality of L2 language learning in the humanities and science secondary classrooms by reviewing the number of student turns at talk, length of student turns, and Initiation-Response-Feedback (IRF) patterns (Sinclair & Coulthard, 1975), as well as types of focus-on-form exchanges (by paying attention to specific grammatical rules and lexical items) (Costa, 2012). They observed 22 lessons from grades 9 and 10. Their talks were classified as simple IRF pattern and extended IRF pattern. An extended IRF pattern is a chain of interaction pattern when an elaborative feedback (F) from the teacher is followed by a further response from I student (R); in addition to a normal IRF sequence. Lo and Macaro (2012) found that when science lessons were teacher-centred, there was a significantly lower proportion of student talk when teacher-student interactions were reduced to IRF sequences with frequent short turns. Teachers also paid less attention to form-focused instruction in L2. The register of science and the availability of other semiotic resources for teaching science could largely reduce the L2 language learning opportunities for students to engage in discussions and interact with their teacher. For example, teachers would draw a diagram to explain the process of photosynthesis. Thus, teachers would spend less time on spoken interactions with students to explain the concepts because they believed that students would understand by looking at the diagram.

An, Macaro, and Childs (2019) focused on the language used by monolingual foreign teachers in early EMI high schools in China. The study examined the extent to which monolingual teachers provided students with Language-Focused Episodes (LFEs) in EMI secondary schools. In a way, the study showed the significance of L1 in supporting students' understanding of the content as foreign teachers did not speak the language. The findings and data collected showed that there were limited explicit language instructions and narrow range of grammatical features used by foreign teachers. The teachers are unable to use L1 as a teaching resource. The study used a mixed-method approach where the time, length, and proportion of LFEs in 30 lessons were collected from schools. Teacher-talk in science is predominantly focused on explanation. Strevens (1980) emphasised that students who failed to master non-science-specific words will encounter difficulties learning science. To conclude, we learn that there are close relationship between the use of students' L1, and the need of L2 exposure, and the teachers' willingness of L1 as a teaching resource.

2.3 Individual teaching strategies of EMI teachers

In many observational studies, researchers have proposed that skilful questioning by teachers can lead to meaningful content-subject learning. For an example, in science classrooms, the meaningful learning requires interactive teaching styles that encourage students to express their views and ask questions, and promote a learning culture based on discussion and other student-centred activities (Yip et al., 2007; Yip, Tsang, & Cheung 2003; Yip & Tsang, 2007; Yip, 1999, 2001, 2004). Teachers might ask a higher-order question to promote students' cognitive skills and synthesise their existing knowledge in order to design a method of investigation (Anderson & Krathwohl, 2001). However, although teachers aim to use these questions in order to stimulate higher-order cognitive thinking, Yip (1999) pointed out that on many occasions such aims were not achieved because the teachers did not make use of students' prior experiences and existing knowledge.

In a recent study, Pun and Macaro (2019) examined the quality of classroom interaction in EMI senior secondary science classrooms. They measured the amount of L1 use, the interaction patterns, and the types of science questions asked by the teachers in both early and late EMI classrooms in Hong Kong with teachers and students from grades 10 and 11. The authors found that more L1 was used in late EMI science lessons, and that more higher-order questions were asked than in early EMI. As a result of these two findings, they concluded that there is a strong relationship between L1 usage frequency and higher-order question usage frequency. Another finding was that greater L1 usage leads to more teacher-student interaction, and vice versa. They found out that the use of L1 produced the kind of interaction that is considered facilitative of students' science learning, including teacher questioning and IRF sequences. Conversely, greater L2 usage resulted in minimal interaction, thus impeding the learning of students. The authors suggest that there are two possible reasons for this. The first one is that teachers do not trust students to have the L2 ability to respond to higher-order questions. Another explanation is that pedagogy has failed to promote academic English learning at the same rate as science content learning, leading teachers to use lower-order questions even when teaching advanced science content. The author notes that while the findings may support the point that more flexibility in the medium of instruction may improve students' mastery of subject content, this conclusion runs contrary to the need of furthering HK students' acquisition of academic English. They conclude that more research is needed to examine the causes of low-quality L2-dominant teaching. They suggest that future research should examine the role of L1 and other factors in determining a smooth transition from non- or partial to full EMI instruction, and should evaluate different amounts of L1 use in EMI programmes. Similarly, Hu and Duan (2019) conducted a study in a China that investigated the types of teacher questions and student responses. The findings suggested that questioning and responding in an EMI classroom was insufficient to achieve goals of facilitating students' learning. In the next section, I will briefly introduce four analytical frameworks that are mentioned in the previously mentioned studies.

2.4 Codeswitching and translanguaging practices in EMI classrooms

The perceived natural part of bilingual interaction is codeswitching. It can be an invaluable support for learning languages when the target language is a barrier to learning (Greggio & Gil, 2007; Reini, 2008). Then and Ting (2011) found that teachers viewed codeswitching as guiding students' understanding of the terminologies and concepts as well as the instructions concerning classroom activities. It is believed that the quality of teacher talk plays a significant role in learners' classroom interactions, supports student talk, and creates a good classroom atmosphere. This establishes a rapport between student and teacher, builds confidence of the learners, and facilitates the processes of learning. Codeswitching to L1 displays teacher authority and reflects bilingual students' feelings from one language to another. Research has shown that pragmatic response in a classroom context is a result of the use of codeswitching.

Lin (2006) described student-teacher codeswitching practices as "local, pragmatic, coping tactics to socioeconomic dominance of English in Hong Kong". In her study, Lin examined classroom interactions in the 1980s and found that in some bilingual classrooms with effective teachers identified by the school principals and the education bureau, interactions promoted higher cognitive gain and conceptual change in students. She concluded that practical bilingual pedagogies could be drawn from these classrooms using the students' available linguistic resources including rich L1 semantic context, code-mixing strategies, and specific IRF patterns in L1 followed by a recap in L2. However, a recent study by Jiang, Zhang, and May (2019) examined the implementation of EMI instruction at a university level and explored the teachers' perceptions and students' motivations in EMI. Drawing on observations of nine classrooms, three post-observation interviews, and a questionnaire, the authors pointed out that although codeswitching may facilitate students' content understanding, the meaning construction and transmission in L2 depended primarily on written texts in PowerPoint slides. As a result, this code-mixing instruction perhaps only developed learners' L1 and L2 receptive skills (reading comprehension, listening), rather than developing their productive skills in L2 (writing and speaking). Turnbull, Cormier, and Bourque (2011) observed a positive relationship between L1 use and students' better oral production in science in term of their complexity. We can observe that L2 groups produced fewer complex utterances in comparison to L1 groups who were able to respond with greater complexity. However, it is advocated against the overuse of L1 and should exercise caution.

While codeswitching is seen as the process of changing two languages, translanguaging is about the speakers producing words in both languages. García (2009) talked about translanguaging as the process by which bilingual students and teachers engage in complex discursive practices in order to "make sense" of and communicate in multilingual classrooms. According to García, translanguaging refers to multiple discursive practices, as seen from the perspective of speakers themselves. Lin and He (2017) investigated translanguaging practices in a Hong Kong secondary school, focusing primarily on South Asian students. It focused on how translanguaging practices can lead to a valuable pedagogical function and identity affirmation. It showed that students encounter various difficulties in communication when English is not their native language. This study shows that students' home languages may serve as resources in pedagogical function in helping them negotiate meaning in content-language integrated learning (CLIL) lessons. The willingness to learn fosters a good classroom atmosphere for teachers and students from various cultural backgrounds, which expands communication resources and creates a creative learning environment. The study analysed Urdu phrases mentioned in students' discussions using transcripts of videos and students' work with translanguaging texts. There were two observations made from the study: first, translanguaging was used in the discussion and it was also used as a peer learning strategy in affirming one's own identity. Second, it showcased their multilingual abilities. This strengthened their identities and empowered students from socially disadvantaged communities.

2.5 Analytical framework 1: classroom discourse model

Sinclair and Coulthard's (1975) discourse analysis model allows researchers to quantify observable patterns in classroom interactions. The model is an indicator to check whether a lesson offers sufficient opportunities for student interaction. This is where the teacher initiates an interaction by asking students a question that is then followed up by their response to the question. Based on students' answers, the teacher provides feedback and acknowledges whether or not the answer was accurate. This allows a broader scope of interaction. An extension of the IRF model is when the teacher provides feedback encouraging students to expand their response (Mortimer & Scott, 2003). When examining the classroom interaction, the extended IRF model was used, with the focus being on the dynamic between teacher and student. While simple IRF patterns generate a level of scaffolding, lessons with an extended IRF generate a higher level of scaffolding.

2.6 Analytical framework 2: pedagogical functions of classroom interaction

Tsui's (1985) framework further described the structural organisations and patterns of turn-taking in classroom talk at three levels: speaker, pattern of interaction, and pedagogical functions, which built on Sinclair and Coulthard's (1975) model as well as others (Barnes, 1969; Flanders, 1970). Under this framework, the first utterances identified are either teachers' or students' in classroom talk. Second, each utterance is then grouped as initiation, response, feedback, or evaluation. Third, according to their pedagogical functions, all the identified utterances are classified in seventeen acts. The seventeen acts are derived from Sinclair and Coulthard's (1975) model, with some acts eliminated based on Tsui's (1985) data. Tsui's seventeen categories provide a series of subsequent classifications of each utterance in classroom interaction by looking into different types of initiation and response provided by the teacher, as well as those by students, in a second-language classroom. Table 2.2 summarises the seventeen-category system for the acts in teacher-student interactions based on the Sinclair and Coulthard (1975) IRF model.

2.7 Analytical framework 3: communicative approaches

Mortimer and Scott's (2003) framework emerged from their analyses in science classrooms. They characterise different talks in science classrooms. It pays attention to how the teacher guides the students in addressing different ideas developed in a lesson. It explores whether the teacher interacts frequently or has limited interactions with the students and whether they consider students' developing ideas in the ongoing lesson. In their framework, Table 2.3 defines the four fundamental types of communication approaches. Depending on the intensity and nature of the talk between teacher and student, each of these approaches can be further divided into two dimensions on a continuum, between dialogic and authoritative talk, and between interactive and non-authoritative talk. These categorizations of the communication approach can inform how the teacher works with students in addressing ideas present in the class at different phases of an observed science lesson.

Table 2.2 The seventeen-category system

	IRF sequence	Acts	Sub-categorisations		
Teacher talk	Initiation (I)	1 Elicit	A Display questions	i	Factual questions
				ii	Yes/No questions
				iii	Reasoning questions
				iv	Explanation questions
			B Genuine questions	i	Opinion
				ii	Information
			C Re-stating elicit		
		2 Direct			
		3 Nominate			
		4 Inform			
		5 Recapitulate			
		6 Frame			
		7 Starter			
		8 Check			
Student talk	Response 1	9 Evaluate	a Encouraging/positive		
		10 Accept	b Negative		
		11 Comment			
		12 Clue			
	Response (R)	13 Reply	a Restricted		
		14 Apologise	b Expanded		
	Initiation (I)	15 Request			
		16 Elicit			
		17 Interrupt			

Source: Tsui (1985)

2.8 Analytical framework 4: teacher questioning style

One important aspect that shapes the teacher-student interaction is the teacher's questioning style. Research done on teaching styles has argued that learner-centred approaches are more desirable compared with teacher-centred approaches. A number of CLIL-context studies explored the different types of questions used by CLIL teachers and studied the relationship between teachers' questions and their pedagogical functions and goals in learning the subject content. For instance, Dalton-Puffer (2007) identified four types of questions used by CLIL teachers: (1) questions for facts, (2) questions for explanation, (3) questions for opinion, and (4) metacognitive questions, which engage the learner in extended dialogues. However, this broad categorisation fails to determine what type of questions or combinations of questions lead to the understanding of content-subject knowledge such as science.

Table 2.3 The four communicative approaches in Mortimer and Scott's (2003) framework

Dialogic	A Interactive-dialogic	B Non-interactive-dialogic
	Teacher listens to and takes student's point of view into account. Together with students, he/she explores different views, generates new meanings, asks real questions, works on different points of view on a science phenomenon.	*Teacher considers different points of view, guiding students to explore, working on different views of a science phenomenon without any turn-taking interactions with the students.*
Authoritative	**C Interactive-authoritative** *Teacher leads students through a great deal of interaction through a sequence of questions and answers to achieve one specific view on a science phenomenon.*	**D Non-interactive-authoritative** *Teacher presents only one specific view of a science phenomenon without any interactions with students.*

Yip (2004) conducted a study to examine the kinds of questions teachers used in Hong Kong science classrooms. He observed 14 biology teachers and identified 10 typical types of questions used by these biology teachers. The identified were ten question types. Yip (2004) provided a useful framework (see Table 2.4) for analysing the science teacher's questions in a Hong Kong science classroom. The aims of these questions are:

1 to check students' understanding of factual information and their ability to explain a science phenomenon (lower-order);
2 to evaluate their higher cognitive skills (higher-order);
3 to investigate students' learning motivation; and
4 to change students' science concepts

See Table 2.4 for a comprehensive review of the different types of question used by science teachers.

Moreover, Yip's (2004) study revealed that science teachers in Hong Kong were skilful in questioning but only used questions with lower cognitive demand that rarely promoted their students' higher-order thinking or created a successful conceptual change in science topics. These lower cognitive questions could not help reducing misconceptions or promote meaningful learning in science. The study also showed that teachers' questioning skills are essential to students' understanding of complex scientific ideas. The quantitative analysis of the teacher's questioning skills can show the

Table 2.4 The nature of the questions asked by the science teacher

Type	Question types	Functions
Lower- order	1 Recalling	Factual information
	2 Explanation	A phenomenon or process
Higher- order	3 Analysis	Breaking down material into its components. This may involve comparing parts and identifying their relationships.
	4 Evaluation	Judging the value and implications of material
	5 Synthesis	Relating existing concepts to construct a new idea or formulate a new pattern
Motivation	6 motivation	Focusing attention; establishing a set for a new topic
Conceptual change	7 Eliciting	Preconceptions or alternative conceptions
	8 Challenging	Students to review and resolve inconsistent ideas
	9 Extending	Guiding students to construct new ideas from existing knowledge
	10 Application	Using learned material in novel and concrete situations

Source: Yip (2004, p. 78)

proportions of different types of questions asked by the teachers and their pedagogical functions in a content-subject classroom.

2.9 Concluding summary

In this chapter, I examined the various aspects of classroom interaction by exploring the roles and significance of the teacher-student dynamic in facilitating classroom learning and how the teachers' interaction allows students to express their ideas. The findings have shown that the usage of L2 is not sufficient in facilitating students' learning, but that L1 is equally important for students' comprehension of the content. The studies showed that the use of L1 practices, such as codeswitching and translanguaging, are important in classroom interaction. This allows students to use their own language in scaffolding learning and translating the contents. The pedagogical strategies for interaction – the IRF model – are used to look at teachers' patterns of discussion in the classroom. Both the higher-order questions and lower-order questions influence students' learning and their functions have been discussed in detail. It showed that student-teacher interaction constitutes a core component of classroom discourse. Overall, the teachers' role in classroom discourse is essential in guiding students' thoughts and facilitating meaning-making.

Learning content-subjects through an unfamiliar second language – English, for instance – could be challenging for both teachers and students. Content-subject teachers generally welcome the adoption of English as the medium of instruction in their classrooms, knowing this may increase students' L2 learning opportunity. However, as discussed in this review, many studies have reported that teachers face numerous issues when teaching through English only in their classrooms (Dearden, 2015; Doiz, Lasagabaster, & Sierra, 2012; Tatzl, 2011). The challenges are lack of teaching skills for integrating both content and language teaching, no appropriate instructional materials for teaching both content and language, and poor English ability. For students, EMI seems to have a negative effect on the quality of content learning because of students' limited English proficiency. According to Cummins (1979), it might take three to five years for students to successfully gain language proficiency to benefit from immersion programmes fully. Teachers should be familiar with EMI instruction strategies and develop the necessary teaching skills to interact with students in extended verbal exchanges. Students need to attain the threshold level of English proficiency, allowing for effective spoken interactions in the classroom. Therefore, it is unclear to what extent EMI may negatively affect the quality of content learning in these classrooms.

Given that EMI classrooms are predicated on benefits accruing from massive exposure to the L2, it is appropriate to ask to what extent English as an instruction language facilitates students' content learning as the prime objective. Researchers interested in exploring classroom interaction in the EMI context mostly studied the differences between the expectation and the reality of the implementation (Lo & Macaro, 2012; Marsh et al. 2000; Pun & Macaro, 2019; Yip et al., 2007). For example, teachers, who are in charge of content teaching, do not perceive themselves as language teachers. It is true that English language teachers play an important role in helping students develop language skills in EMI, but content teachers might lack attention to the teaching of English. Thus hindering students' academic achievements, as shown in classroom observation studies. If content teachers have received sufficient teaching training for EMI that prepares them for teaching in the English environment and are equipped with effective pedagogical skills that allow them to develop students' disciplinary language skills, students should attain functional academic literacy and succeed in their academic studies (Anstrom, 1999; Al-Ansari, 2000; Short, 2002). Professional development programmes for front-line EMI teachers should be in place within schools so that teachers can be equipped with the necessary pedagogical skills to integrate both content and language (Othman & Mohd, 2009). EMI teachers train their English communication skills in these professional development programmes to increase their confidence. They are taught about the specific scaffolding skills in delivering both content and language through English to L1 students of different levels.

By providing an evidence-based, pedagogically focused analysis of teacher and student classroom interactions and their perceptions, researchers of EMI classroom interactions shed light on ways to improve the quality of instructional practices in different EMI classrooms in Hong Kong and in similar contexts around the world.

References

Al-Ansari, S. (2000). Sheltered curricular exposure and unsheltered extra-curricular exposure as factors influencing the development of academic proficiency in ESL. *IRAL: International Review of Applied Linguistics in Language Teaching, 38*(3), 175.

An, J., Macaro, E., & Childs, A. (2019). Language focused episodes by monolingual teachers in English medium instruction science lessons. *Journal of Immersion and Content-Based Language Education, 7*(2), 166–191.

Anderson, L. W., & Krathwohl, D. R. (2001). *A taxonomy for learning teaching and assessing. A revision of Bloom's taxonomy of educational objectives.* New York: Longman.

Anstrom, K. (1999). Preparing secondary education teachers to work with English language learners: Mathematics. *NCBE Resource Collection Series, 14.*

Barnes, D. (1969). The language of the secondary classroom. In D. Barnes, J. N. Britton, & H. Rosen (Eds.), *Language, the Learner and the School.* Harmondsworth: Penguin.

Chan, J. Y. H. (2013). A week in the life of a "finely tuned" secondary school in Hong Kong. *Journal of Multilingual and Multicultural Development, 34*(5), 411–430.

Chapin, S. H., & Anderson, N. C. (2013). *Talk moves: A teacher's guide for using classroom discussions in math, Grades K-6.* Math Solutions.

Coleman, J. A. (2006). English-medium teaching in European higher education. *Language Teaching, 39*(1), 1–14.

Costa, F. (2012). Focus on form in ICLHE lectures in Italy: Evidence from English-medium science lectures by native speakers of Italian. *AILA Review, 25*(1), 30–47.

Creswell, J. W. (2003). A framework for design. In *Research design: Qualitative, quantitative, and mixed methods approaches* (pp. 9–11). Thousand Oaks, CA: Sage.

Cummins, J. (1979). Linguistic interdependence and the educational development of bilingual children. *Review of Educational Research.*

Dalton-Puffer, C. (2007). *Discourse in content and language integrated learning (CLIL) classrooms* (Vol. 20). John Benjamins Publishing.

Dearden, J. (2015). *English as a medium of instruction – A growing global phenomenon.* Retrieved from https://www.britishcouncil.org/sites/default/files/e484_emi_-_cover_option_3_final_web.pdf

Doiz, A., Lasagabaster, D., & Sierra, J. M. (Eds.). (2012). *English-medium instruction at universities: Global challenges.* Multilingual Matters.

Flanders, N. A. (1970). *Analyzing teacher behavior.* Addison-Wesley P. C.

Galloway, N., Kriukow, J., & Numajiri, T. (2017). Internationalisation, higher education and the growing demand for English: An investigation into the English medium of instruction (EMI) movement in China and Japan. *ELT Research Papers, 17*(2).

García, O. (2009). *Bilingual education in the 21st century: A global perspective.* Malden, MA and Oxford, UK: Wiley-Blackwell.

Greggio, S., & Gil, G. (2007). Teacher's and learner's use of code-switching in the English as a foreign language classroom: A qualitative study. *Linguagem & Ensino, 10*(2), 371–393.

Ho, C., Wong, J. K. Y., & Rappa, N. A. (2019). Supporting students' content learning in Biology through teachers' use of classroom talk drawing on concept sketches. *Journal of Immersion and Content-Based Language Education, 7*(2), 233–260.

Hu, G., & Duan, Y. (2019). Questioning and responding in the classroom: A cross-disciplinary study of the effects of instructional mediums in academic subjects at a Chinese university. *International Journal of Bilingual Education and Bilingualism, 22*(3), 303–321.

Jiang, L., Zhang, L. J., & May, S. (2019). Implementing English-medium instruction (EMI) in China: Teachers' practices and perceptions, and students' learning motivation and needs. *International Journal of Bilingual Education and Bilingualism, 22*(2), 107–119.

Lemke, J. L. (1990). *Talking science: Language, learning and values.* Norwood, NJ: Ablex Publishing Corporation.

Lin, A. M. (2006). Beyond linguistic purism in language-in-education policy and practice: Exploring bilingual pedagogies in a hong kong science classroom. *Language and Education, 20*(4), 287–305.

Lin, A. M. Y. (2012). Multilingual and multimodal resources in genre-based pedagogical approaches to L2 English content classrooms. *English–A Changing Medium for Education, 79*, 103.

Lin, A. M. Y., & He, P. (2017). Translanguaging as dynamic activity flows in CLIL classrooms. *Journal of Language, Identity and Education, 16*(4), 228–244.

Lo, Y. Y. (2014). Collaboration between L2 and content subject teachers in CBI: Contrasting beliefs and attitudes. *RELC Journal, 45*, 181–196.

Lo, Y. Y., & Lo, E. S. C. (2014). A meta-analysis of the effectiveness of English-medium education in Hong Kong. *Review of Educational Research, 84*(1), 47–73.

Lo, Y. Y., & Macaro, E. (2012). The medium of instruction and classroom inter-action: Evidence from Hong Kong secondary schools. *International Journal of Bilingual Education and Bilingualism, 15*(1), 29–52.

Macaro, E. (2018). *English Medium Instruction.* Oxford: Oxford University Press.

Macaro, E., Curle, S., Pun, J., An, J., & Dearden, J. (2018). A systematic review of English medium instruction in higher education. *Language Teaching, 51*(1), 36–76.

Marsh, H. W., Hau, K. T., Kong, C. K. (2000). Late immersion and languag e of instruction in HK high schools-achievement Growth in Language and Nonlan-guage subjects. *Harvard Educational Review, 70*(3), 302–346.

McDonough, S., & McDonough, S. (1997). Research methods as part of English language teacher education. *English Language Teacher Education and Develop-ment, 3*(1), 84–96.

Mortimer, E., & Scott, P. (2003). *Meaning making in secondary science classrooms.* Berkshire, England: Open University Press.

Othman, J., & Mohd. S. R. (2009). Challenges of using English as a medium of instruction: Pre-service science teachers' perspective. *The Asia-Pacific Education Researcher, 18*(2), 307–316.

Pun, J. & Macaro, E. (2019). The effect of first and second language use on question types in English medium instruction science classrooms in Hong Kong. *Interna-tional Journal of Bilingual Education and Bilingualism, 22*(1), 64–77.

Reini, J. (2008). The functions of teachers' language choice and code-switching in EFL classroom discourse (Master's thesis). University of Jyvaskyla, Finland. Retrieved from https://jyx.jyu.fi/bitstream/handle/123456789/18639/1/URN_NBN_fi_jyu-200806115441.pdf.

Short, D. (2002). Language learning in sheltered social studies classes. *TESOL Jour-nal, 11*(1), 18–24.

Sinclair, J., & Coulthard, M. (1975). *Towards an analysis of discourse.* Oxford: Oxford University Press.

Strevens, P. (1980). The paradox of individualized instruction: It takes better teach-ers to focus on the learner. In H. B. Altman & C. V. James (Eds.), *Foreign lan-guage teaching: Meeting individual needs.* Oxford: Pergamon.

Swain, M., & Lapkin, S. (2000). Task-based second language learning: The uses of the first language. *Language Teaching Research, 4*(3), 251–274.

Tatzl, D. (2011). English-medium masters' programmes at an Austrian university of applied sciences: Attitudes, experiences and challenges. *Journal of English for Academic Purposes, 10*(4), 252–270.

Then, D. C. O., & Ting, S. H. (2011). Code-switching in English and science class-rooms: More than translation. *International Journal of Multilingualism, 8*(4), 299–323.

Tsui, A. B. M. (1985). Analysing input and interaction in second language class-rooms. *RELC Journal, 16*(1), 8–32.

Turnbull, M., Cormier, M., & Bourque, J. (2011). The first language in science class: A quasi-experimental study in late French immersion. *The Modern Language Journal, 95*, 182–198.

Vygotsky, L. S. (1997). *The collected works of LS Vygotsky: Problems of the theory and history of psychology* (Vol. 3). Springer Science & Business Media.

Wannagat, U. (2007). Learning through L2 – Content and language integrated learning (CLIL) and English as medium of instruction (EMI). *International Journal of Bilingual Education and Bilingualism, 10*(5), 663–682.

Yip, D. Y. (1999). Implications of students' questions for science teaching. *School Science Review, 81*(294), 49–53.

Yip, D. Y. (2001). Promoting the development of a conceptual change model of science instruction in prospective secondary biology teachers. *International Journal of Science Education, 23*(7), 755–770.

Yip, D. Y. (2004). Questioning skills for conceptual change in science instruction. *Journal of Biological Education, 38*(2), 76–83.

Yip, D. Y., Coyle, D., & Tsang, W. K. (2007). Medium of instruction on science students: Instructional activities in science lessons. *Education Journal, 35*(2), 77–107.

Yip, D. Y., & Tsang, W. K. (2007). Evaluation of the effects of the medium of instruction on science learning of Hong Kong secondary students: Students' self-concept in science. *International Journal of Science and Mathematics Education, 5*(3), 393–413.

Yip, D. Y., Tsang, W. K., & Cheung, S. P. (2003). Evaluation of the effects of medium of instruction on the science learning of Hong Kong secondary students: Performance on the science achievement test. *Bilingual Research Journal, 27*(2), 295–331.

3 Trends in using questionnaires for EMI research

Suggestions for future improvements

Samantha M. Curle and Ali Derakhshan

Abstract

Following the overall trend regarding the predominance of the questionnaire as a data collection method in behavioral and social sciences, it has been identified as the most widely applied instrument in EMI research. This extensive use originates from the many advantages that questionnaire use brings to researchers in terms of its practicality, economy, feasibility, time, efficiency, versatility, ease of construction, and data analysis. The recurrent and widespread use of questionnaires (often accompanied by qualitative data collection methods) in EMI research has proliferated in studies across the world. Such studies differed in their focus ranging from: EMI practice, experience of EMI, attitudes towards EMI, and the successful enactment of EMI. Other aspects measured by using questionnaires include those examining EMI in relation to other variables such as the efficiency of language development programmes, the use of adaptation strategies, and language use anxiety. Despite this extensive use of questionnaires, most EMI researchers have fallen short of applying their knowledge of questionnaire design theory to questionnaire development and enactment. As a consequence, this directly and negatively affects the accuracy of the data obtained through this instrument. As a review study, this chapter attempts to sketch out the use of questionnaires in EMI research, with specific focus on the challenges and potential risks in design and implementation. Stepwise suggestions to enhance the robustness of the psychometric properties that these scales measure are also presented throughout this chapter.

Keywords: EMI research, questionnaire design and implementation, psychometric properties, EMI questionnaires

DOI: 10.4324/9781003025115-3

3.1 Questionnaires and their significance in EMI

Typically, the aim of survey studies is to explore the characteristics of a population by examining a selected sample of that group. Even though survey data can be obtained via structured interviews, questionnaires are known as the most widely used data collection method for this purpose. Questionnaires are one of the most prevalent methods of gathering data regarding opinions, beliefs, or attitudes of a large number of people. This has often been used to examine various lines of inquiry in second language research (Mackey & Gass, 2005). The data collected through questionnaires are typically quantitative, although this instrument may include open-ended items that are more qualitative/exploratory in nature.

Questionnaires have been one of the most extensively employed data collection methods in the behavioral and social sciences. As pointed out by Dörnyei (2007), questionnaires are very versatile and easy to construct instruments through which one is able to collect a large amount of information in a short time. Furthermore, the data obtained through the instrument can be processed fairly easily. In other words, questionnaires are very efficient in terms of the amount of effort, time, energy, and financial resources demanded of researchers in deploying and processing them. Also, due to the unobtrusive nature of this instrument, respondents may feel unrestricted in their responses, expressing their feelings, thoughts, and opinions bluntly and without hedging.

In the field of applied linguistics, the only instrument used more widely than a questionnaire is the language proficiency test (Dörnyei, 2003). In EMI research, the questionnaire dominates as a method of data collection. Through the questionnaire, EMI researchers can find access to learners' or teachers' attitudes, beliefs, or perceptions regarding EMI learning or their reactions to EMI classes, instruction, and activities. Typically, variables in the area of education are not directly observable, and as such, the questionnaire is a suitable instrument to achieve this goal (Ary, Jacobs, Razavieh, & Sorenson, 2006).

To address the main concern of the chapter, despite this extensive application of questionnaires in EMI research, there seems to be a lack of sufficient knowledge and awareness regarding questionnaire design and processing theory among researchers in the field. As pointed out by Dörnyei (2007), in general, such a negligence of essential considerations in design and employment of questionnaires is not uncommon in applied linguistics research. It is incorrect to assume that any person with a bit of word processing software knowledge and common sense can develop a robust questionnaire. Unfortunately, because of this false perception, weak questionnaires are very prevalent in scientific research undertakings. In EMI, in particular, there exist a large number of questionnaires that have failed to have sufficient and well-documented validity and reliability properties (Curle, 2018). Very few researchers report conducting a pilot study, Cronbach's alpha statistics, or for example, or ask an expert panel for feedback on questionnaire item working (Macaro, Curle, Pun, An, & Dearden, 2018).

To fix this problem, EMI researchers are advised to apply their knowledge of questionnaire theory to questionnaire design and application. In this regard, Dörnyei (2007) evinces that for developing a fine questionnaire, researchers must go through the essential stepwise process of: drawing up an item pool, initial piloting of the item pool, final piloting, item analysis, and post hoc item analysis. These considerations should be taken seriously because without them producing invalid and unreliable data from a questionnaire that is ill constructed is inevitable.

Moreover, it should be noted that despite their efficiency and wide application, questionnaires normally provide "thin" descriptions of the phenomena under investigation as they are incapable of presenting the intricacies of individual contexts (Mackey & Gass, 2005). This is why EMI researchers have tended to combine this instrument with qualitative data collection methods providing "thick" descriptions of the target phenomena. Such studies appear in the form of mixed-method designs integrating both quantitative and qualitative data in a single study (Creswell, 2012).

In the remainder of the chapter, we will deal in more detail with questionnaire development and use in EMI and the serious deficiencies found in this respect. But before that, a brief sketch of the current research topics and design trends of using questionnaires in the field of EMI studies will be presented.

3.2 Current trends in EMI

Promotion of internationalisation in higher education in recent years has led to the prevalence of EMI in tertiary-level education as the non-anglophone world has incorporated EMI instead of first language as the instruction medium in colleges and universities. This in turn has resulted in the expansion of research on the topic, particularly with applied linguists using EMI as an interesting research phenomenon in the 21st century (Macaro, 2019). The evidence for the extensive research in this area comes from studies worldwide, with specific reference to those conducted in Europe (e.g., Dearden & Macaro, 2016), the Middle East (e.g., Al Zumor, 2019), and Asia (e.g., Goodman, 2014; Kim & Tatar, 2018).

Within Asia, the pattern of EMI implementation growth has been most dramatic in China and Japan where government actively encourages EMI enactment in both public and private universities. This deliberate promotion by governments also resulted in the escalation of research foci on EMI with

Chinese (e.g., Jiang, Zhang, & May, 2016; Xie & Curle, 2020) and Japanese (e.g., Curle, 2018; Galloway & Ruegg, 2020) higher education systems.

Research to date has brought into the spotlight various aspects of EMI such as its acceptance (e.g., Orr & Annous, 2018), practice (e.g., Khan, 2013), successful implementation (e.g., Belhiah & Elhami, 2015), policy, ideology (Rahman & Singh, 2019), opportunities, challenges, adjustments (e.g., Goodman, 2014), perceptions of/attitudes/beliefs towards EMI (e.g., Banks, 2018; Başıbeka et al., 2014; Kırkgöz, 2009), as well as experiences of EMI (e.g., Kim & Tatar, 2018).

Many studies have highlighted EMI in relation to various teacher-, student-, or education-related variables, including academic skill support provision for university students (Galloway & Ruegg, 2020), students' learning needs and motivations (Jiang et al., 2016), teachers' needs regarding EMI (Banks, 2018), students' socialisation experiences and academic discourse (Sultana, 2014), efficiency of language development programmes (Margić & Vodopija-Krstanović, 2018), students' academic skills and language proficiency (Rose, Curle, Aizawa, & Thompson, 2019), self-efficacy beliefs (Thompson, Aiwaza, Curle, & Rose, 2019), employment of adaptation strategies (Yang et al., 2019), language use anxiety (Levine, 2003), students' year of study, university type, gender (Macaro & Akincioglu, 2018), teachers' native/non-native English-speaking background (Inbar-Lourie & Donitsa-Schmidt, 2019), and computer technology (Hu & Hsu, 2016).

Within the research studies in EMI, questionnaires have been the most widely used data collection method. This recurrent use may be due to the apparent advantages of questionnaire employment in any field of enquiry as outlined previously such as collecting data from a large number of participants in a relatively short period of time. To recapitulate these advantages, questionnaires are popular for their easy construction, versatility, readily processable and quickly attained data, and unobtrusiveness (Dörnyei, 2007). However, in spite of the fact that questionnaires are capable of collecting a very large amount of information at a fast speed, they fail to provide a deep understanding of the phenomena at hand. To compensate for this shortcoming, many researchers prefer triangulation of various data sources and data collection methods to reach a more complete picture of the issue at hand (Creswell, 2012). The tendency to mix different methods from both quantitative and qualitative research paradigms is quite conspicuous in empirical studies in EMI and will be explained in more detail in the forthcoming section.

3.3 Current research designs in EMI

As mentioned earlier, despite the dominance of the questionnaire instrument in EMI research, its use has often been accompanied by other sources of data in the form of mixed-method research design studies. In particular, such studies amalgamated quantitative data collection instruments such as interventions, surveys, or questionnaires with qualitative ones like interviews, focus groups, observation, document analysis, or content analysis. EMI studies adopting mixed-method research design include but are not limited to those conducted by Costa and Coleman (2013), Banks (2018), Margić and Vodopija-Krstanović (2018), Kırkgöz (2009), Khan (2013), Rose et al. (2019), Thompson et al. (2019), Yang et al. (2019), Belhiah and Elhami (2015), Turhan and Kırkgöz (2018), Chang, Kim, and Lee (2015), Evans and Morrison (2016), Al Zumor (2019), Hu and Hsu (2016), Inbar-Lourie and Donitsa-Schmidt (2019), Kim and Tatar (2018), Kim and Yoon (2018), and Xie and Curle (2020).

However, a large portion of these studies are open to criticism with regard to the robustness of the questionnaires they have used as they failed to examine the essential validity and reliability qualities for both self-developed and adopted scales used in their respective studies. Most of them did not even bring the questionnaire designed in their studies and, regarding the use of questionnaires adopted from other studies, many failed to give reference to the original source from which the scale was taken. Therefore, the results of such studies are not easily acceptable, as instruments with no rigor and robustness cannot be accurate measures of the constructs under investigation.

Even for Tung, Lam, and Tsang's (1997) 21-year-old EMI scale, developed on a very large-scale sample in Hong Kong, no pilot study was reported. Instances of more recent studies being unclear in reference to the psychometric properties of their EMI instruments or failing to provide thorough information regarding the EMI scales are those conducted by Başıbeka et al. (2014), Banks (2018), Evans and Morrison (2016), Margić and Vodopija-Krstanović (2018), Kırkgöz (2009), Khan (2013), Kym and Kym (2014), Yang et al. (2019), Belhiah and Elhami (2015), Chang et al. (2015), Costa and Coleman (2013), Evans and Morrison (2016), Al Zumor (2019), Inbar-Lourie and Donitsa-Schmidt (2019), Kim and Tatar (2018), Kim and Yoon (2018), Macaro et al. (2018), Galloway and Ruegg (2020), Xu (2017), and Sultana (2014).

In a study examining perceptions of university lecturers in the engineering department of state universities in Turkey towards EMI, Başıbeka et al. (2014) used a questionnaire which was developed originally by Tung at al. (1997). It consisted of 30 Likert-scale-type items measuring schoolteachers' perceptions towards EMI in Hong Kong. There are two criticisms regarding the use of this scale in this study. First, it was designed and validated on a group of schoolteachers not university lecturers. Second, the scale was developed in the school context of China, not Turkey. Although Başıbeka et al. (2014) mentioned that they modified some items of the scale in order for it to better fit the educational context in Turkey, they did not go through any rigorous validation process such as reporting Cronbach's alpha. They also reported a reliability estimate of .91 for the scale, but they were not clear whether this estimation was the one reported in Tung et al.'s (1997) study or calculated in their own study.

Similarly, to explore a group of 60 university lecturers' attitudes and needs regarding EMI in the higher education system of Spain, Banks (2018) used various data collection instruments including a questionnaire containing 100 items measuring lecturers' pedagogical and language viewpoints and needs with regard to EMI. Although the study was, to some extent, robust in the sense that it examined the issue from various angles through triangulation of various data sources, it did not provide a detailed explanation of the instruments of their study. For instance, although they reported that the quantitative data was collected by means of a questionnaire, no information was given regarding the scale such as its name, when and by whom it was developed, and the number of items it contained. It is necessary for researchers to report all phases of their studies in detail so that future researchers can easily replicate their studies. Sultana (2014) also explored the impact of EMI on socialisation experiences and academic discourse of 115 freshmen in five Bangladeshi universities by administering interviews and a self-developed questionnaire. Although it was mentioned that the development of the questionnaire was informed by other previously developed EMI questionnaires, reliability and validity reports were lacking.

Margić and Vodopija-Krstanović (2018) investigated the efficiency of a language development programme for 60 university content teachers concerning EMI in the higher education system of Croatia through various data collection means that included an adopted EMI scale of four open-ended and five Likert-type questions regarding the content, usefulness, teaching methods, and course instructors of the programme; the areas and the extent to which they were satisfied/dissatisfied with them; and potential recommendations for improving its quality and usefulness. A Cronbach's alpha reliability of .91 was reported for the scale as a whole. The crucial information disregarded and not mentioned about the scale were its name, its first-hand reliability, developer's name(s), and the date of its development.

Likewise, Kırkgöz (2009) investigated both university professors' and students' perceptions of the success of foreign language teaching with regard to students' academic needs within an EMI context of a Turkish university. Among other instruments, an EMI questionnaire was developed, informed by Kırkgöz's (2009) needs analyses, consisting of 19 four-point Likert-type items in addition to open-ended questions pertaining to various academic tasks as well as the four language skills of listening, writing, reading, and speaking that were required for students in their respective university programmes. However, no reference was given to how the scale was designed and developed or whether it enjoyed acceptable psychometric properties of validity and reliability.

Khan (2013) explored postgraduate students' and university professors' perceptions of EMI policy and practice in two universities in Pakistan. Generation of data was done by employing both quantitative and qualitative data collections approaches. Along with interviews, two pertinent questionnaires for students and teachers were developed – each containing three kinds of factual, behavioral, and attitudinal Likert-type closed questions. These questions assessed the themes in students'/teachers' perceptions of EMI, the significance of English, influence of English as the instructional medium, uses of English, and Pakistani English. Explanations were provided regarding the language of the scale, its length and layout, the time required for answering it, the process of writing initial items, drawing up an item pool, choosing and sequencing items, writing instructions and examples for the scale, scale translation into a target language, the piloting phase, and item analysis. However, they failed to report the reliability measures of their instruments.

Kym and Kym (2014) scrutinised 364 students' perceptions of EMI in university context in Korea through developing a questionnaire measuring students' language skills and knowledge perspectives of the present EMI courses they had already taken. By going through a process of first extracting questionnaire items from earlier relevant studies and then revising the items to fit the study context, 26 items were finalised. The Cronbach's alpha reliability estimates reported for the satisfaction and comprehension components of the scale were .90 and .87, respectively. However, the questionnaire did not go through any process of validation, which is a fundamental step of questionnaire development.

In a case study in China, Yang et al. (2019) explored the adaptation strategies adopted and challenges confronted by 74 teachers, 188 students, and three faculty administrators in implementing EMI in a Chinese medical programme. Data were obtained from questionnaire responses, focus group interviews, and test scores, as well as teachers' questionnaire responses. The questionnaires used in this study were developed by the researchers themselves in both Chinese and English versions. The items of which were informed by initial interview findings of the study. The surveys included a section asking about students' demographic information and general opinions on EMI as well as 51 (teacher's version) and 44 (student's version) six-point Likert scale measuring the two groups' perceptions of EMI in their specific educational context. However, it was unclear whether the essential validation process, piloting phase, and reliability estimates were performed on the questionnaires.

Belhiah and Elhami (2015) investigated the effectiveness of implementing EMI in higher education system of the United Arab Emirates by focusing on its practice in six universities. Similar to other researchers in this line of enquiry, they also developed their data collection instruments of survey and email interview scales themselves. Regarding the validation of the survey, they gave the initial draft to some experts to obtain their feedback and made revisions accordingly. Subsequently, they piloted the instrument with a group of 100 students, and made some further changes to the wording of the items in addition to eliminating some unnecessary items. After that they gave the survey to some experts again and finalised the instrument. Having reached acceptable validity, the survey was translated into Arabic and changes were made by two university professors regarding item style and clarity. Despite this validity report, no statement regarding the reliability of the scale was presented.

Xu (2017) probed Chinese university students' perspectives towards EMI and English language through a self-developed five-point Likert scale containing both open- and close-ended questions. The scale was created in two versions, one for EMI programme students and another for non-EMI programme students. It measured English learning attitudes, English attitudes regarding teaching, and attitudes towards English. Reliability estimates for both versions of the scale revealed only that the first component did not have acceptable reliability (Cronbach α = .66 and .58 for EMI and non-EMI versions, respectively) and, therefore, was not further discussed in the article. More importantly, however, no validation process was explained for the development of the questionnaire.

Last but not least, Chang et al. (2015) proposed and then examined the effectiveness of a language support programme for EMI in the higher education system of Korea which aimed to develop fundamental communication, English writing, and presentations skills of university students. The programme was implemented in the form of workshops and tutoring sessions. To check the effectiveness of the workshops, questionnaires including both close- and open-ended questions providing data about students' demographic information, previous experience of EMI course, views towards the usefulness of the workshops, and specific English skills covered in them, as well as recommendations for workshop improvement were implemented. Similarly, the efficacy of the tutoring sessions was examined through students' and tutors' responses to pertinent surveys. Like the previously mentioned studies, they did not report any validity or reliability estimation for the employed scales.

Studies that are exceptions in this area, as they reported both reliability and validity for their self-designed or adopted EMI instruments, are those of Macaro and Akincioglu (2018), Levine (2003), Xie and Curle (2020), Turhan and Kırkgöz (2018), and Ellili-Cherif and Alkhateeb (2015).

Furthermore, to address this gap in the EMI literature regarding the lack of a well-designed, valid, reliable, and rigorous questionnaire, Curle

(2018) designed and developed a scale (in two versions: a professor version and a student version) assessing university students' and lecturers' attitudes towards EMI in the context of Japan. Preparation of the questionnaire occurred in three phases: phase 1 – open-ended interviews with both university lecturers and students; phase 2 – semi-structured interviews with a smaller portion of the participants, pilot study feedback from participants, and piloting of the questionnaire; and phase 3 – completion of the questionnaire with all of the participants. The professor version and the student version were respectively validated qualitatively and quantitatively. For the student version, internal consistency was ensured through assessing the Cronbach's alpha coefficient while construct validity was gauged through running Principal Component Analysis (PCA), Exploratory Factor Analysis (EFA), and Confirmatory Factor Analysis (CFA). The results of validation processes and reliability estimations revealed that the finalised questionnaire, named the Japanese English Medium of Instruction Attitude Scale (JEMIAS), enjoyed acceptable psychometric properties.

All in all, considering the dramatic growth in EMI practice and research worldwide on the one hand and the unattended deficiencies in the area of EMI questionnaire development and implementation being ever-present in EMI-related empirical investigations on the other hand, there is an urgent need for, first, provision of stepwise suggestions for enhancing psychometric properties of such scales, and second, enactment of these guidelines by EMI researchers in their future research undertakings. In the rest of the chapter, useful and essential recommendations for improving qualities of survey instruments are put forward. In conclusion, some directions for future research in EMI are presented.

3.4 Suggestions for improving the quality of questionnaires in EMI

When using a questionnaire in a study, whether self-developed or adopted/adapted from another source, researchers should provide some preliminary information regarding their instrument to their readers.

In cases where researchers adopt a scale from another source in their study, they should bring necessary information regarding the original study in which the scale was developed. In this regard, they should provide the name of the researcher(s) who developed the scale and the date on which it was developed. They should also state the exact name of the scale and report its reliability as estimated by scale developer(s)'s themselves. They should also re-estimate and report the scale reliability in their respective studies. However, for adopted scales with no changes made to them, there is no need to re-examine validity and just reporting that the scale enjoys satisfactory validity as assessed and reported by the developers of the scale is acceptable. In addition, researchers are to provide information regarding the language of the scale, the number of its items, its layout, the constructs underlying it, its scoring procedure, and the amount of time needed to answer it.

In situations where researchers have adopted and further adapted a previously developed scale in their study, along with the information outlined previously, they should also go through a pilot study and re-examine the validity of the scale to ensure that the changes they have made did not negatively affect its validity. They should also clearly explain what modifications they have made to the scale. Furthermore, if they have translated the scale into another language or have transformed the scale from one version to another (for instance, from "teacher version" to a "student version"), it is advised that they present the adapted version in the Appendix section of their paper.

Finally, when researchers develop and design a new EMI scale in their study, they are required to fully explain the processes undertaken for questionnaire development and include details regarding writing initial items, receiving expert judgements, drawing up an item pool, choosing and sequencing items, writing instructions and examples for the scale, doing the piloting phase, and doing post hoc item analysis. They should also go through rigorous validity and reliability checks. Construct validity of the scale can be assessed through running various statistical measures such as PCA, EFA, and CFA, while internal reliability of the scale can be assessed through running the Cronbach's alpha coefficient procedure. Only when it is approved via this procedure that the scale enjoys good psychometric properties. Then it can be used as a reliable and valid data collection instrument by other researchers in the future. At the end, researchers should choose an identifiable name for their scale and provide information regarding its language, length and layout, scoring procedure, and the time required for answering it. The full scale should be also provided in the Appendix section of the paper so that replication studies can be carried out.

3.5 Concluding remarks

As discussed throughout this chapter, following the worldwide trend in research in behavioral and social sciences, in general, and applied linguistics, in particular, the questionnaire has been the most widely applied data collection instrument in EMI research. This extensive acceptability and use can be ascribed to the versatility, ease of construction, and unobtrusiveness, as well as easy and fast data collection and processing capabilities of the questionnaire instrument (Dörnyei, 2007). However, despite its recurrent use, questionnaire design and application in EMI research has been faced with serious problems as many EMI researchers have failed to apply knowledge of questionnaire theory to questionnaire design and application, and consequently, the scales have failed to contain sufficient and well-documented validity and reliability properties. It is predicted that the growth in EMI research will occur at an accelerating rate in the future due to the apparent influence of internationalisation promotion in higher education in the non-anglophone world (Macaro, 2019). But unless such studies utilise instruments with acceptable rigor and robustness, their results cannot be taken as accurate measures of the constructs under investigation.

Besides this issue, the existence of a large number of studies in the area of EMI clearly represents the fast expansion of EMI research and practice on a global scale. As pointed out by Macaro et al. (2018), EMI has been enacted in the higher education systems of 54 countries so far. However, despite this rapid rise in the enactment of EMI in higher education in Europe, the Middle East, and some Asian countries, the dearth of EMI research and practice in some geographical areas such as Latin America, Africa, and other parts of Asia – such as Iran – is quite evident. To fill this research lacuna and follow the worldwide, upward trend in the provision of EMI, researchers from such under-researched areas are encouraged to take the initiative in conducting research on various aspects of EMI in their respective countries.

Furthermore, the scope of EMI research can be expanded if researchers incorporate other unexplored but important teacher/learner variables into EMI research. To mention but a handful of potential learner/teacher variables, we can refer to autonomy, agency, creativity, willingness to attend English classes, engagement, burnout, critical thinking, self-monitoring, reflective thinking, identity, emotional intelligence, empowerment, immediacy, ambiguity tolerance, well-being, self-regulation, credibility, and effectiveness. Another avenue for future research is the study of pragmatic competence and its significance in EMI to follow studies such as those of Taguchi (2014), Herraiz-Martinez and Alcón-Soler (2019), and Carrió-Pastor (2020) who took the lead in this regard.

All things considered, it can be concluded that through utilising questionnaire development theory more properly and accurately in the design and application of questionnaire instruments, EMI researchers can potentially witness an impressive enhancement in the quality of the results they provide to the future EMI research and practice worldwide.

References

Al Zumor, A. Q. (2019). Challenges of using EMI in teaching and learning of university scientific disciplines: Student voice. *International Journal of Language Education*, *3*(1), 74–90.

Ary, D., Jacobs, L. C., Razavieh, A., & Sorenson, C. K. (2006). *Introduction to research in education* (8th ed.). Belmont, CA: Wadsworth.

Banks, M. (2018). Exploring EMI lecturers' attitudes and needs. *EPiC Series in Language and Linguistics, 3*(1), 19–26.

Başıbeka, N., Dolmacı, M., Cengiz, B. C., Bürd, B., Dileke, Y., & Karaf, B. (2014). Lecturers' perceptions of English medium instruction at engineering departments of higher education: A study on partial English medium instruction at some state universities in Turkey. *Procedia – Social and Behavioral Sciences, 116,* 1819–1825.

Belhiah, H., & Elhami, M. (2015). English as a medium of instruction in the Gulf: When students and teachers speak. *Language Policy, 14*(1), 3–23.

Carrió-Pastor, M. L. (2020). English as a medium of instruction: What about pragmatic competence? In M. L. Carrió-Pastor (Ed.), *Internationalising learning in higher education: The challenges of English as a medium of instruction* (pp. 137–153). Cham: Palgrave Macmillan.

Chang, J., Kim, W., & Lee, H. (2015). A language support program for English-medium instruction courses: Its development and evaluation in an EFL setting. *International Journal of Bilingual Education and Bilingualism, 20*(5), 510–528.

Costa, F., & Coleman, J. A. (2013). A survey of English-medium instruction in Italian higher education. *International Journal of Bilingual Education and Bilingualism, 16*(1), 3–19.

Creswell, J. W. (2012). *Educational research: Planning, conducting, and evaluating quantitative and qualitative research* (4th ed.). Boston, MA: Pearson.

Curle, S. (2018). Developing and validating a Japanese English medium of instruction attitude scale (JEMIAS). *The Journal of Asia TEFL, 15*(4), 1195–1221. Retrieved from www.iris-database.org/iris/app/home/detail?id=york:936114&ref=search

Dearden, J., & Macaro, E. (2016). Higher education teachers' attitudes towards English medium instruction: A three-country comparison. *Studies in Second Language Learning and Teaching, 6*(3), 445–486.

Dörnyei, Z. (2003). *Questionnaires in second language research: Construction, administration, and processing.* Mahwah, NJ: Lawrence Erlbaum Associates, Inc., Publishers.

Dörnyei, Z. (2007). *Research methods in applied linguistics.* New York: Oxford University Press.

Ellili-Cherif, M., & Alkhateeb, H. (2015). College students' attitude toward the medium of instruction: Arabic versus English dilemma. *Universal Journal of Educational Research, 3*(3), 207–213.

Evans, S., & Morrison, B. (2016). Adjusting to higher education in Hong Kong: The influence of school medium of instruction. *International Journal of Bilingual Education and Bilingualism, 21*(8), 1016–1029.

Galloway, N., & Ruegg, R. (2020). The provision of student support on English Medium Instruction programmes in Japan and China. *Journal of English for Academic Purposes, 45,* 1–35.

Goodman, B. A. (2014). Implementing English as a medium of instruction in a Ukrainian University: Challenges, adjustments, and opportunities. *International Journal of Pedagogies and Learning, 9*(2), 130–141.

Herraiz-Martinez, A., & Alcón-Soler, E. (2019). Pragmatic outcomes in the English-medium instruction context. *Applied Pragmatics*, *1*(1), 68–91.

Hu, W., & Hsu, S. (2016). *The effectiveness of using computer technology to strengthen English as a medium of instruction courses in Taiwan tertiary education.* The 2016 3rd International Conference on Systems and Informatics (ICSAI 2016).

Inbar-Lourie, O., & Donitsa-Schmidt, S. (2019). EMI lecturers in international universities: Is a native/non-native English-speaking background relevant? *International Journal of Bilingual Education and Bilingualism*, *23*(3), 301–313.

Jiang, L., Zhang, L. J., & May, S. (2016). Implementing English-medium instruction (EMI) in China: Teachers' practices and perceptions, and students' learning motivation and needs. *International Journal of Bilingual Education and Bilingualism*, *22*(2), 107–119.

Khan, H. I. (2013). *An investigation of two universities' postgraduate students and their teachers' perceptions of policy and practice of English medium of instruction (EMI) in Pakistani universities* (PhD thesis). University of Glasgow. Retrieved from http://theses.gla.ac.uk/4451/

Kim, E. G., & Yoon, J. (2018). Korean science and engineering students' perceptions of English medium instruction and Korean-medium instruction. *Journal of Language, Identity & Education*, *17*(3), 182–197.

Kim, J., & Tatar, B. (2018). A case study of international instructors' experiences of English-medium instruction policy in a Korean university. *Current Issues in Language Planning*, *19*(4), 1–15.

Kırkgöz, Y. (2009). Students' and lecturers' perceptions of the effectiveness of foreign language instruction in an English-medium university in Turkey. *Teaching in Higher Education*, *14*(1), 81–93.

Kym, I., & Kym, M. H. (2014). Students' perceptions of EMI in higher education in Korea. *The Journal of Asia TEFL*, *11*(2), 35–61.

Levine, G. S. (2003). Student and instructor beliefs and attitudes about target language use, first language use, and anxiety: Report of a questionnaire study. *The Modern Language Journal*, *87*(3), 343–364.

Macaro, E. (2019). Exploring the role of language in English medium instruction. *International Journal of Bilingual Education and Bilingualism*, *23*(3), 263–267.

Macaro, E., & Akincioglu, M. (2018). Turkish university students' perceptions about English Medium Instruction: Exploring year group, gender and university type as variables. *Journal of Multilingual and Multicultural Development*, *39*(3), 256–270.

Macaro, E., Curle, S., Pun, H., An, J., & Dearden, J. (2018). A systematic review of English medium instruction in higher education. *Language Teaching*, *51*(1), 36–76.

Mackey, A., & Gass, S. (2005). *Second language research: Methodology and design.* Mahwah, NJ: Lawrence Erlbaum Associates, Inc., Publishers.

Margić, B. D., & Vodopija-Krstanović, I. (2018). Language development for English-medium instruction: Teachers' perceptions, reflections and learning. *Journal of English for Academic Purposes*, *35*, 31–41.

Orr, M., & Annous, S. (2018). There is no alternative! Student perceptions of learning in a second language in Lebanon. *Journal of Language and Education*, *4*(1), 79–91.

Rahman, M. M., & Singh, M. K. M. (2019, in press). Language ideology of English-medium instruction in higher education: A case study from Bangladesh. *English Today*, 1–7.

Rose, H., Curle, S., Aizawa, I., & Thompson, G. (2019, in press). What drives success in English medium taught courses? The interplay between language proficiency, academic skills, and motivation. *Studies in Higher Education*, 1–14.

Sultana, S. (2014). English as a medium of instruction in Bangladesh's higher education: Empowering or disadvantaging students? *The Asian EFL Journal Quarterly*, *16*(1), 11–52.

Taguchi, N. (2014). Pragmatic socialization in an English-medium university in Japan. *International Review of Applied Linguistics in Language Teaching*, *52*(2), 157–181.

Thompson, G., Aiwaza, I., Curle, S., & Rose, H. (2019, in press). Exploring the role of self-efficacy beliefs and learner success in English Medium Instruction. *International Journal of Bilingual Education and Bilingualism*. doi:10.1080/136 70050.2019.1651819

Tung, P., Lam, R., & Tsang, W. K. (1997). English as a medium of instruction in post-1997 Hong Kong: What students, teachers, and parents think. *Journal of Pragmatics*, *28*(4), 441–459.

Turhan, B., & Kırkgöz, Y. (2018). Motivation of engineering students and lecturers toward English medium instruction at tertiary level in Turkey. *Journal of Language and Linguistic Studies*, *14*(1), 261–277.

Xie, W., & Curle, S. (2020, in press). Success in English medium instruction in China: Significant indicators and implications. *International Journal of Bilingual Education and Bilingualism*, 1–13.

Xu, H. (2017). College students' attitudes toward English-medium instruction and the English language. In J. Zhao & L. Q. Dixon (Eds.), *English-medium instruction in Chinese universities: Perspectives, discourses, and evaluation* (pp. 59–75). New York: Routledge.

Yang, M., O'Sullivan, P. S., Irby, D. M., Chen, Z., Lin, C., & Lin, C. (2019). Challenges and adaptations in implementing an English-medium medical program: A case study in China. *BMC Medical Education*, *19*(15), 1–8.

4 Teachers' cognitions on motivational practice in medium of instruction settings

Lessons learned in using stimulated recall interviews

Mairin Hennebry-Leung

Abstract

This chapter critically reflects on the constraints and affordances experienced in the implementation of stimulated recall interviews (SRIs) used to explore teachers' cognitions on motivational language teaching practice across Hong Kong secondary schools that are adopting a diverse medium of instruction (MoI). The study in which this chapter is grounded adopted a multi-variate perspective to examine the interplay between MoI, as a key feature of the learning context, and learners' language learning motivation (LLM). The study gathered data on students' language learning motivational orientations, their language learning self-efficacy, and their personality traits in addition to gathering data on teachers' practices and their cognitions on motivational teaching practice. A key element of the study was to understand the extent to which MoI, as a key feature of the learning environment, interacted with learner motivation and teacher practice. This was theoretically important because it increased recognition of the role context plays in shaping motivation and of the existing gaps in the field with relation to teacher motivational practice. Informing a richer understanding of Hong Kong school learners' LLM was also of significance for policy and practice.

4.1 Background of the study

Educational models of content-based instruction (CBI) have seen rapid expansion across sociocultural contexts (Dearden, 2014). This expansion has been accompanied by increasing research attention to the role of MOI in content and language learning. Oddly, given the significance of LLM in predicting language attainment (Lamb, 2017), little research has been done to

DOI: 10.4324/9781003025115-4

understand the interactions between MOI and LLM. Even studies that have examined motivation in the context of MOI are limited in what they can tell us about LLM, since they have tended to adopt theoretical frameworks better suited for understanding general academic motivation (see Lo & Lo, 2014). Within LLM research much work has been done to develop models that represent the processes inherent to language learning and the ways these interact with social context and with learner's psychological traits as well as their identity. Two such theories in particular have defined the field of LLM over the past six decades. In quite distinct yet overlapping ways, Gardner's socio-educational model (2010) and Dörnyei's (2009) L2 Motivational Self System combine the cognitive, affective, and behavioural elements of motivation, while also acknowledging the interplay between language learning and identity development.

While some have argued that CBI necessarily provides a motivational context for L2 learning as students need the L2 for successful engagement in content subjects (Genesee, 1991; Pérez Cañado, 2018; Swain & Lapkin, 2005), the extent to which this is so is as yet under-researched, with most investigations of CBI contexts focusing on academic motivation or on motivation for content subject learning in areas such as mathematics or science (e.g., Fung & Yip, 2014). An important feature of any teaching and learning context is the teacher and their practice. If, indeed, CBI settings are by definition motivational for language learning then teachers' motivational practices should vary from one MOI context to another. This implies that teachers possess the theoretical and professional knowledge for enacting robust motivational practice and have the expertise necessary to adapt their practices in response to the teaching context. And yet, little is known about teachers' cognitions on motivational teaching practice in the context of CBI. Studies that examine teachers' cognitions on motivational teaching practice in any learning context are rare.

Current LLM research and theory recognises the impact of macro-, meso-, and micro-contexts of learning. MOI is a key feature of the meso-context that is shaped directly by the macro-context and in a bi-directional relationship with the micro-context; it is a significant contextual feature. In a context like Hong Kong, success in English language learning has considerable implications for future life possibilities, thus understanding the extent to which MOI impacts LLM is significant in terms of understanding educational equity. Do students across different MOIs exhibit different levels and orientations of LLM? Do teachers across different MOIs vary their practices to respond to imbalances in the learning context? Do teachers' cognitions on LLM demonstrate an awareness of context and of the need for responsive pedagogy? These were questions at the heart of our study.

4.2 Motivational teaching practice

Many of the motivational strategies proposed in the literature are rooted in theoretical advances in L2 motivation (e.g., Allison & Halliwell, 2002; Dörnyei & Kubanyiova, 2014; Teimouri, 2017). A number of studies have provided descriptive accounts of what teachers do to motivate their learners, as well as of teacher and student perceptions of the effectiveness of these strategies (e.g., Dörnyei & Csizér, 1998; Cheng & Dörnyei, 2007; Ruesch, Bown, & Dewey, 2012). Teachers' self-reports of the motivational strategies they use have been relied on heavily (e.g., Sugita McEown & Takeuchi, 2010). Notwithstanding the potential limitations of self-report, the teacher's voice is an essential component of research in this area. Other studies have employed observations (e.g., Guilloteaux & Dörnyei, 2008; Papi & Abdollahzadeh, 2012; Moskovsky, Alrabai, Paolini, & Ratcheva, 2013). Each of these methods brings with it a number of affordances and constraints, which are well reviewed in numerous research methods textbooks (see Dörnyei, 2001; Paltridge & Phatiki, 2015; Mackey & Gass, 2016, to name a few). However, knowing what teachers do is only part of the picture and perhaps not the most important part. The development of sustainable effective motivational practice requires understanding *why* teachers do what they do. Kubanyiova (2006) found that despite enthusiastically participating in training specifically targeted at the development of motivational language teaching practice and recognising the value of the strategies they were taught, teachers did not adopt these strategies in their subsequent teaching. These findings were echoed by Muñoz & Ramirez (2015) among Colombian university language centre teachers. While these studies found that deliberately focusing on motivational practice in teacher training did not result in changed motivational practice in the classroom, Feryok and Oranje (2015) reported that language teachers did consistently consider the motivational dimension while focusing on other aspects of pedagogy. Lamb (2017) argues that researchers need to engage with the teacher cognition literature to conduct qualitative research that sheds light on why and how teachers adopt and adapt motivational teaching strategies. He suggests that methods such as stimulated recall (SR) techniques may enable close observation of classroom events and an understanding of teachers' "thinking-in-action".

4.3 Teacher cognition

As a result of years of experience as language learners, teachers bring implicit but deeply ingrained ideas and beliefs about language teaching and learning processes to the classroom and their classroom practices (Freeman, 2002). On this often superficial basis, they generate everyday concepts of language teaching and learning (Johnson & Golombek, 2011). Effective teacher learning requires that teachers develop an interplay between everyday concepts and scientific concepts, themselves rooted in up-to-date research and theories and tested through their own systematic observation and theorisation (Johnson & Golombek, 2011). This aligns with the notion that teacher education should focus on teachers within the sociocultural contexts of their school, and the activity of teaching (Freeman & Johnson, 1998). Echoing this, Tsui (2011) highlights the need to support teachers in drawing relationships between their learning of theories on their courses and their own specific contexts and experiences. In this light, exploring language teachers' personal theories and their interaction both with public theory and with their own practices is crucial for understanding motivational teaching practice as it unfolds in the classroom context.

Recognising and giving voice to teachers' cognitions is fundamental for effective teacher preparation for motivational language teaching and allows teachers' front-line expertise and experience to contribute to the field of LLM. Understanding the relationship between teachers' declarative knowledge of motivational teaching and their procedural classroom knowledge contributes to the development of a robust and authentic framework of motivational language teaching practice.

4.4 The study

The parent study examined language learning motivation across eleven Hong Kong secondary schools, adopting a mixed methods design. The teacher phase of the study sought to document the motivational practices teachers engaged with and to explore English language teachers' cognitions on motivational language teaching practice.

A mixed methods approach was adopted to explore teachers' cognitions and practices, using SRIs grounded in semi-structured lesson observations. The observations served a dual purpose: allowing us, on the one hand, to document the strategies teachers used and, on the other hand, informing our understanding of teachers' cognitions. Field notes were also taken during the observations and these notes contributed to the shape and direction of the interviews. We felt strongly that observation data would be useful in providing researchers with insight into the wider teaching and learning contexts of the student and teacher participants. This contextual understanding was deemed particularly important since a key focus of the parent study was to understand the extent to which MOI interacted with LLM and the extent to which teachers varied their practices in response to this feature. Furthermore, all lessons observed were video-recorded and the relevant lessons were used as stimuli for the

SRIs. During the recordings the video camera was trained on the teacher so that students' faces did not appear on the recording; this issue is discussed later. The recordings also provided the material for the two SRIs that were conducted with each of the teachers. These SRIs are the main focus of this chapter.

4.4.1 Participants

Participants in the teacher phase were all English language teachers at Hong Kong government subsidised schools required to follow the standardised curriculum. Of the eleven schools participating in the parent study, five agreed to participate in the teacher phase as well. Two teachers in each of these schools took part in three observations and two SRIs, as well as one semi-structured interview, during one school term.

A number of considerations needed to be taken into account in sampling the teachers. Principal among these were:

1   One aim of the study was to shed light on the relationship between student motivation and teacher practice. For this reason, the teacher participants had to be those who were teaching students who were in the parent study.

2   Since the study sought to understand variations in motivation and motivational practice across MOI settings, our teacher sample needed to include teachers from all three MOI settings. Similarly, we decided to include a cross-section of grades and motivational levels, in order to allow for the emergence of variations that may be attributed to these factors.

3   Our study needed to be sensitive to the role of context at school and class level but also at the broader macro level. In Hong Kong learners' socioeconomic status (SES) can play a significant role in determining the future opportunities students may have access to and the extent to which these opportunities may necessitate the use of English. This has huge implications for students' motivation to learn English and as such, our teachers, like our students, needed to come from schools reflecting a cross-section of the SES range.

4   The level of commitment required for the teacher phase was high given the demands already placed on teachers and all the more given that participating teachers would already be facilitating the participation of their students in the parent study. It was important that we secured participation from teachers who were able to commit to the full study, including observations, SRIs, and the semi-structured

interview. Through negotiations and with the promise of school-based reports on the study, as well as a professional development session for all participating teachers, we were able to secure the participation of ten teachers (two in each school), resulting in the following sample:

School and class data for each teacher

School	MOI	Form	Teacher	ELLM mean	SES
1	EMI	1	Ms Hong	3.15	High
	EMI	4	Mr Akbar	2.83	Mid
2	CMI	3	Ms Wong	3.56	High
	CMI	4	Ms Au	2.59	Low
3	MMI	1	Ms Kong	3.10	High
	MMI	4	Ms Lo	2.40	Low
4	EMI	1	Ms Szeto	3.03	High
	EMI	3	Ms Tse	2.85	Mid
5	MMI	3	Ms Chan	2.83	Mid
	MMI	4	Ms Lee	2.50	Low

Note: EMI = English Medium Instruction; CMI = Chinese Medium Instruction; MMI = mixed-medium instruction; ELLM = English language learning motivation; SES = socioeconomic status

4.4.2 *Stimulated recall interviews*

SRIs are a form of retrospection. Retrospection requires respondents to verbalise their though-processes subsequent to completing an activity or a mental operation. Because the respondent has to retrieve information from long-term memory, the amount of time that lapses between completing the activity and conducting the introspection is an important variable that impacts the validity of the data; the accuracy of recall diminishes as the length of cognitive processes increases (Ericsson, 2002).

   Much as immediate recall is complicated to implement in interaction studies (Mackey & Gass, 2016), it is also challenging to implement in studies of teacher practice where to do so would mean disrupting the lesson and would in itself change the dynamic of the classroom, thus threatening the validity of the findings. In such cases the SRI becomes particularly useful, since it takes place some time after the targeted thought processes. In order to help participants retrieve their thoughts at the time of the occurrence, a stimulus is provided (Mackey & Gass, 2016). The stimulus supports the participant's recall by offering a reminder of the event and facilitating retrieval of the thought processes at the time. Of all the introspective techniques,

Ericsson (2002) argues that SRIs are the least reactive because the targeted thought processes are not affected in any way by the procedure, particularly if participants were not aware during the task that they would be asked to provide a running commentary afterwards. This is easily understood if we contrast SRIs with think-alouds that are often used to examine thought processes during reading. In a think-aloud participants are expected to ver- balise their thought processes simultaneously as they complete the reading task. Beyond the cognitive challenge this can present, there is also a high probability that the very fact of having to verbalise their thoughts will itself interrupt the targeted thought processes and pose a threat to validity. No matter the nature of the stimulus, the time lapse for SRIs inevitably impacts on the quality of the recall (Dörnyei, 2001).

In the case of our study the stimulus was the video of the lesson they were being asked to comment on. This use of stimulus allowed us to pre- serve a stronger relationship between the teachers' verbalised cognitions and the context within which they had been formed and exercised. It also diminished the degree to which teachers were required to decontextualise their verbalisations. Given the centrality of context in our study we felt that SRIs were particularly well suited for our purposes and rendered greater integrity to the research. We could have considered using semi-structured interviews that offer greater scope than SRIs for pursuing further avenues of interest emergent during the conversation between interviewer and inter- viewee. However, we felt that SRIs, where a recording of a lesson acts as the stimulus, enable greater specificity and offer the possibility of pinpoint- ing particular incidents for closer inspection. The use of a stimulus also offers a common starting point for recollecting what actually took place in the lesson, though the interpretation of such events may differ between the interviewer and the interviewee. In addition, we felt that an important advantage of SRIs is the greater control they offer the interviewee, some- thing we return to later.

Gass and Mackey (2017) provide an extensive review of and guide to the use of stimulated recall. We found a number of their considerations useful and refer to these here. The first consideration relates to the strength of the stimulus used. Gass (2001) points to an important distinction between recall of an event and reflection on an event, with the latter being more likely than the former if there is a delay between the event and the SRI. In cases where there is a delay between the event and the SR, Gass and Mackey (2017) advise the use of more than one source (e.g., a recording accompanied by a transcript) to strengthen the stimulus. In our case, we conducted all SRIs on the same day as the observed lesson, usually straight after the lesson or at most a couple of hours later. Thus, video-recordings served as a sufficiently strong stimulus and indeed video-recordings provide not only a visual but also an audio stimulus, helping to strengthen the recall. This point leads to the third recommendation, which is that SRIs should be conducted as soon as possible after the event. The more time that passes between the event and the recall, the greater the risk of diminished recall and of participants saying what they think the researcher wants to hear or trying to provide plausible or reasonable explanations for their behaviours during the event even if these explanations are not accurate.

Also relating to the strength of the stimulus, however, is our second consideration: what should the recording capture? We would have liked to take in the whole classroom so that student behaviour as well as teacher behaviour could be captured. Student behaviour was not our focus but clearly understanding it allows for a clearer sense of the effects of teacher behaviour. Unfortunately, gaining consent for this proved unfeasible and schools were concerned that parents would not be happy to have their children's faces to appear on the video. They, therefore, indicated that they would prefer us to record the lessons with the camera trained on the teacher and not capture the students. As far as the observation data was concerned we could construct an accurate picture of events in the classroom by combining the video-recordings with the researchers' field notes and the structured observation schedule they employed during the observations. Omitting students from the visual, however, had implications for the nature of the stimulus. The audio-recording was complete, since the voices of the students had been picked up, but the visual stimulus could be considered incomplete. There was little evidence that this impacted the teachers' recall during the SRIs, perhaps in part because of their immediacy, but it is certainly a possibility and needs to be considered as a limitation of our study. The teachers' vision in the classroom is primarily focused on the students; this is what they see when they are in the process of teaching. A recording trained on the teacher presents a different visual and in that sense only partially recreates what the teacher experienced.

Our third consideration was the degree of structure in the SRI, which Gass and Mackey (2017) suggest relates to the research questions. In our case our research question was exploratory; we wanted to know how teachers thought about language learning motivation and their own motivational practice; what the teachers chose to highlight from viewing the video-recording would in itself provide insight into their cognitions. We required enough structure for a focused SRI but not too much that the scope of the recall would be constrained by our own understandings of motivational practice or what we considered to be significant in the recording. Rather than pre-selecting excerpts of the lessons for the stimulus, the interviewer and interviewee watched the entire lesson, with the teachers being encouraged to stop the recordings at points they considered significant and reducing the degree of researcher interference with the data generated. Typically, semi-structured interviews see the interviewer pre-determining key areas for exploration, asking guiding questions and determining when to move from one topic to another. This gives the interviewer major control of the conversation. In an SRI the interviewer needs to strike a balance between, on the one hand, ensuring that the data generated is relevant to the research and, on the other hand, exercising minimal control in order to avoid influencing the data. This brings us to the issue of prompts, our fourth consideration.

While it is normal to pre-prepare prompts for SRIs, they are not without their issues (Dempsey, 2010). Providing too much guidance may lead the participant to provide the data they think the researcher wants to get, threatening the validity of the data. Conversely, prompts that are too minimal run the risk that participants will provide reflection and analysis of the video that is unrelated to the focus of the research (Dempsey, 2010; Lyle, 2003) or may forget to verbalise their thoughts. The balance is difficult to strike.

Pirie (1996) questions whether videos used for SRIs are in themselves the data or the facilitators of the data. In our study this was a particularly pertinent question because the videos served a dual function. On the one hand they served as data given that one of our research aims was to provide an account of the teachers' motivational practices. On the other hand, they served as the facilitator in that for the purposes of the SRIs our interest was not so much in what happened in the lesson as in how the teacher analysed and reflected on it. The process of gathering and analysing data, however, did not really allow for these to be teased apart. The research schedule meant that observations were followed by a SRI, followed by more observations, followed by another SRI. This sequence undoubtedly meant that what the researchers observed in one lesson would influence the understanding they brought to the SRI and the SRI would influence their interpretation of subsequent observations. In one sense this may be desirable as researchers need to develop a keen understanding of the contexts they are exploring and this understanding should inform their interpretation of the data; removing context is rarely desirable and certainly not in researching teachers' cognitions. Alternately, however, the extent to which this understanding might result in prompts that draw attention to aspects of the lesson the researcher considers important but the participant does not can be problematic and indicative of researcher bias. The prompts used were as follows:

1   What makes you say that?
2   Was that your original plan?
3   Why did you choose that specific strategy?
4   Do you often do that in your class? How effective do you find it to be?

By the time the SRIs were conducted, our participants were well-informed about the focus of the study, such that staying on topic was less problematic. Nevertheless, the prompts proved essential for encouraging participants to keep verbalising their thoughts rather than waiting for the researcher to ask direct questions. This leads to our fourth consideration. Verbalisation of thought processes is not intuitive and requires practice. Providing some form of trial run for participants is important. Similarly, researchers who have not previously conducted SRIs need to receive training. Our research assistants piloted the SRIs and used these as the basis for training sessions and ongoing exchange with a team lead. Notwithstanding the benefits of training, a further concern emerged relating to the content of the SRIs. We explored teachers' cognitions on motivation and yet some struggled to provide explicit systematic reflection and analysis of either their learners' motivation or their own motivational practices as manifested in the lesson. Subsequent semi-structured interviews suggested that some participants had received very little structured input on motivational practice during their teacher preparation programmes, while professional development on this topic was even rarer. As such, their existing knowledge had been gleaned from informal channels, in an ad-hoc fashion, and this was reflected in the way they talked about or at times struggled to talk about their practices.

The fifth and final consideration relates to the language of SRIs. Most SRI participants are likely to do their thinking in their first language, particularly in time-pressured environments like a classroom. Conducting the SRI in an L2 potentially imposes an additional barrier to accessing the "true" thought processes. Given that the lessons observed were English language lessons and that for some teachers this involved a high degree of L2 use, conducting the SRIs in L1 would have meant asking participants to use L1 to discuss an event which had occurred primarily in the L2. The fact that our research involved teachers across different MOI settings made this consideration perhaps more important. Our observations suggested that teachers in EMI schools were more likely to manifest a higher degree of L2 use in their English classes than those in CMI or MMI schools, thus creating variability across the settings. In light of this dichotomy and given that our researchers spoke both English and Cantonese sufficiently well, we gave teachers the option of using L1 or L2 during the SRIs.

After all the observations and SRIs were completed, a semi-structured interview was conducted with each of the teacher participants, exploring a range of background questions that would provide context for the data emerging from the SRIs. These interviews were conducted after observations and SRIs had all been completed, to avoid the possibility that they might influence the SRI data.

4.4.3 Data analysis

Much can be said about how to analyse data emerging from SRIs and again we point readers to Gass and Mackey's (2017) detailed discussion. Due to space constraints we highlight two particularly salient points emerging from our study.

The participants were able to talk about motivation and motivational practice in abstract, but some struggled to generate systematic and reflective accounts of specific episodes within the video-recordings. Some also found it challenging to relevant identity. This in itself suggested that cognitions were more abstract than concrete, but it also made the process of teasing out the teachers' awareness of specific motivational practices or their ability to relate theory to practice particularly complex. It was difficult to know whether teachers' difficulties in verbalising their thought processes were because their cognitions on motivational practice were limited or because of difficulties inherent in the data collection tool, or a mixture of both. While we gathered rich data relating to teachers' general cognitions on LLM, data relating to specific episodes was less rich and more difficult to make sense of.

Gass and Mackey (2017) question whether it is more or less helpful for the researchers gathering the data and analysing it to have insight into the wider context. The more the researcher knows about the wider context within which the data was gathered, the more possibility there is for this to influence their interpretations of the data and bias the analysis. On the other hand, not having this knowledge can lead to misunderstanding or incomplete understandings that also influence the analysis. In our study, our researchers were familiar with the research context, since they had been visiting the schools for the purposes of gathering student data and conducting classroom observations. Given the nature of our study, it was preferable that the researchers did have this familiarity, since this allowed them not only to better understand what the teachers referred to when they discussed their practices but also to triangulate the data gathered through SRIs with what they themselves had observed. It was also important, however, because our cameras had had to be trained on the teacher rather than taking in the whole class. In this case, what the researchers had been able to observe during the lesson became invaluable context.

4.5 Lessons learned

Research is always a learning process and this study was no exception. Some of the lessons learned emerged as a result of limitations in the study and others resulted from confirmation of decisions in designing and conducting the study. We leave our readers with those that we considered the most valuable:

1   Stimulated recalls are challenging at the best of times, so:

    a   Researchers conducting the SRIs need to have training beyond the normal piloting of methods.
    b   Participants need to have training.

2   Given the challenge that SRIs in and of themselves present for participants, if the topic being researched is one where they may struggle to verbalise their thoughts, for instance teachers' cognitions on an aspect of pedagogy they may not have reflected on much, it may be worth considering an alternative data collection method. Another possibility would be to conduct a survey on the topic prior to the SRI to gauge the degree of understanding, but this has obvious implications for the validity of the SRI and needs to be carefully done so as not to prime participants in such a way that threatens the validity of the data.

3   Think carefully about the nature of the recording. Where possible a full recording that captures all aspects of the event is ideal. If this can't be done, then make sure that the audio in the recording is clear and consider taking good field notes. These two strategies can go a long way to fill in any gaps.

4   Consider whether context data will be helpful for understanding and interpreting the SRI data more fully. This will depend on the nature of your study, but it's difficult to imagine where context would not be important. Because we were looking at teacher cognition and because our interest was also on the role of context in shaping and directing motivation, contextualising the SRIs was paramount. This context was also useful as a form of triangulation. To provide a broader context you may wish to consider observations that generate data for analysis, and/ or conducting semi-structured interviews that address broader issues that may interact with the SRI data.

5   Establishing inter-rater reliability in the coding and interpretation of the data is important and the conversations necessary in this process are helpful for the overall development of the study. Make sure you develop a form of inter-rater reliability for the data analysis. Inter-rater reliability may be influenced by differences in experience and expertise of the researchers involved, which may in turn lead to different interpretations of events. This is not a problem in itself but something that may require more conversations before you can come to a shared agreement.

6   All research would be better with hindsight. There is no such thing as a perfect study, however shiny it may look when published. Good researchers are those that are willing to recognise limitations in their research, to try things differently, to listen to the voices of others (practitioners/participants/colleagues/the wider scholarly community), and to keep learning.

References

Allison, J., & Halliwell, S. (2002). *Challenging classes: Focus on pupil behaviour.* London: Centre for Information on Language Teaching and Research.

Cheng, H., & Dörnyei, Z. (2007). The use of motivational strategies in language instruction: The case of EFL teaching in Taiwan. *Innovation in Language Learning and Teaching, 1*(1), 153–174. doi:10.2167/illt048.0.

Dearden, J. (2014). *English as a medium of instruction – a growing global phenomenon.* British Council. British Council. Retrieved from http://english agenda.britishcouncil.org/books-resource-packs/english-medium-instruction-%E2%80%93-growing-global-phenomenon

Dempsey, N. P. (2010). Stimulated recall methodology in ethnography. *Qualitative Sociology, 33*, 349–367. doi:10.1007/s11133-010-9157-xN.

Dörnyei, Z. (2001). *Motivational strategies in the language classroom.* Cambridge: Cambridge University Press.

Dörnyei, Z. (2009). The L2 motivational self system. *Motivation, Language Identity and the L2 Self, 36*(3), 9–11.

Dörnyei, Z., & Csizér, K. (1998). Ten commandments for motivating language learners: Results of an empirical study. *Language Teaching Research, 2*(3), 203–229. doi:10.1177/136216889800200303.

Dörnyei, Z., & Kubanyiova, M. (2014). *Motivating learners, motivating teachers. Building vision in the language classroom.* Cambridge, UK: Cambridge University Press.

Ericsson, K. A. (2002). Towards a procedure for eliciting verbal expression of non-verbal experience without reactivity: Interpreting the verbal overshadowing effect within the theoretical framework for protocol analysis. *Applied Cognitive Psychology, 16*(8), 981–987.

Feryok, A., & Oranje, J. O. (2015). Adopting a cultural portfolio project in teaching German as a foreign language: Language teacher cognition as a dynamic system. *The Modern Language Journal, 99*(3), 546–564. doi:10.1111/modl.12243

Freeman, D. (2002). The hidden side of work: Teacher knowledge and learning to teach. *Language Teaching, 35*, 1–13. doi:10.1017/S0261444801001720.

Freeman, D., & Johnson, K. E. (1998). Reconceptualizing the knowledge-base of language teacher education. *TESOL Quarterly, 32*(3), 397–417. doi:10.2307/3588114.

Fung, D., & Yip, V. (2014). The effects of the medium of instruction in certificate-level physics on achievement and motivation to learn. *Journal of Research in Science Teaching, 51*(10), 1219–1245. doi:10.1002/tea.21174

Gardner, R. C. (2010). *Motivation and second language acquisition: The socio-educational model.* New York: Peter Lang Publishing.

Gass, S. M. (2001). Innovations in second language research methods. *Annual Review of Applied linguistics, 21*, 221–232.

Gass, S. M., & Mackey, A. (2017). *Stimulated recall methodology in applied linguistics and L2 research.* London: Routledge.

Genesee, F. (1991). Second language learning in school settings: Lessons from immersion. In Allan G. Reynolds (Ed.), *Bilingualism, multiculturalism, and second language learning.*

Georgiou, S. I. (2012). Reviewing the Puzzle of CLIL. *ELT Journal, 66*(4), 495–504. doi:10.1093/elt/ccs047.

Guilloteaux, M. J., & Dörnyei, Z. (2008). Motivating language learners: A classroom-oriented investigation of the effects of motivational strategies on student motivation. *TESOL Quarterly, 42*(1), 55–77. doi:10.1002/j.1545-7249.2008.tb00207.x.

Hennebry-Leung, M. (2020). Teachers' cognitions on motivating language learners in multilingual Hong Kong. In W. Tao & I. Liyanage (Eds.), *Multilingual education yearbook: Teacher education and multilingual contexts.* Cham: Springer.

Hennebry-Leung, M., & Gao, X. (2018). Interactions between medium of instruction and language learning motivation. *International Journal of Bilingual Education and Bilingualism, 0*(0), 1–14.

Hennebry-Leung, M., & Hu, X. (2020). Examining the role of the learner and the teacher in language learning motivation. *Language Teaching Research, 0*(0), 1–27.

Johnson, K. E., & Golombek, P. R. (2011). A sociocultural theoretical perspective on teacher professional development. In K. E. Johnson & P. R. Golombek (Eds.), *Research on second language teacher education* (pp. 1–13). New York: Routledge.

Kubanyiova, M. (2006). Developing a motivational teaching practice in EFL teachers in Slovakia: Challenges of promoting teacher changes in EFL contexts. *TESL-EJ: Teaching English as a Second or Foreign Language, 10*(20), 17.

Lamb, M. (2017). The motivational dimension of language teaching. *Language Teaching, 50*(3), 301–346.

Lo, Y. Y., & Lo, E. S. C. (2014). A meta-analysis of the effectiveness of English-medium education in Hong Kong. *Review of Educational Research, 84*(1), 47–73.

Lyle, J. (2003). Stimulated recall: A report on its use in naturalistic research. *British Educational Research Journal, 29*(6), 861–878.

Mackey, A., & Gass, S. M. (2016). *Second language research: Methodology and design.* Abingdon: Routledge.

Moskovsky, C., Alrabai, F., Paolini, S., & Ratcheva, S. (2013). The effects of teachers' motivational strategies on learners' motivation: A controlled investigation of second language acquisition. *Language Learning, 63*(1), 34–62. doi:10.1111/j.1467-9922.2012.00717.x.

Muñoz, A., & Ramirez, M. (2015). Teachers' conceptions of motivation and motivating practices in second-language learning: A self-determination theory perspective. *Theory and Research in Education, 13*(2), 198–220.

Paltridge, B., & Phatiki, A. (2015). *Research methods in applied linguistics.* London: Bloomsbury.

Papi, M., & Abdollahzadeh, E. (2012). Teacher motivational practice, student motivation, and possible L2 selves: An examination in the Iranian EFL context. *Language Learning, 62*(2), 571–594. doi:10.1111/j.1467-9922.2011.00632.x.

Pérez Cañado, M. L. (2018). The effects of CLIL on L1 and content learning: Updated empirical evidence from monolingual contexts. *Learning & Instruction, 57*, 18–33. doi:10.1016/j.learninstruc.2017.12.002.

Pirie, S. E. (1996). *Classroom video-recording: When, why and how does it offer a valuable data source for qualitative research?*

Ruesch, A., Bown, J., & Dewey, D. P. (2012). Student and teacher perceptions of motivational strategies in the foreign language classroom. *Innovation in Language Learning and Teaching, 6*(1), 15–27. doi:10.1080/17501229.2011.562510.

Sugita McEown, M., & Takeuchi, O. (2010). What can teachers do to motivate their students? A classroom research on motivational strategy use in the Japanese EFL context. *Innovation in Language Learning and Teaching, 4*(1), 21–35. doi:10.1080/17501220802450470.

Swain, M., & Lapkin, S. (2005). The Evolving Sociopolitical Context of Immersion Education in Canada: Some Implications for Program Development. *International Journal of Applied Linguistics, 15*(2), 169–186. doi:10.1111/j.1473-4192.2005.00086.x.

Teimouri, Y. (2017). L2 selves, emotions, and motivated behaviors. *Studies in Second Language Acquisition, 39*(4), 681–709.

Tsui, A. B. M. (2011). Teacher education and teacher development. In E. Hinkel (Ed.), *Handbook of research in second language teaching and learning* (Vol. 2, pp. 21–40). New York: Routledge.

5 Researching assessment in EMI

Yuen Yi Lo

Abstract

With the increasing popularity of English Medium Instruction (EMI) in bilingual and multilingual contexts, plenty of research has been conducted to examine students' achievements, classroom interaction and, more recently, teacher education. However, research focusing on assessment issues in EMI remains scarce. Considering the fact that students are inevitably assessed of their English knowledge in conjunction with their content knowledge in EMI assessment, there are concerns about whether EMI students' learning progress is accurately measured. Other related questions include how to design valid assessment in EMI and how to better support students to tackle assessment in EMI. Hence, there is an urgent need to address the research gap on EMI assessment. This chapter will report a research project exploring the assessment practices in EMI. With a validated analytical framework, the research team analysed cognitive and linguistic demands of over 8,500 questions sampled from school textbooks, school-based examinations, and university entrance public examinations. The text/question analysis employed in this study revealed interesting patterns in different types of assessments and across different grade levels. These not only show the integral role played by language in EMI assessments but also illuminate valid assessment design and effective pedagogy in EMI.

5.1 Project overview and context

In EMI programmes, students learn content subjects (e.g., science, history, mathematics) in English, which is often their second/foreign language (L2). It is also often the case that EMI students will be assessed of their content knowledge in English. This raises the question about the validity and fairness of assessment in EMI, issues which have been under-researched (Massler, Stotz, & Queisser, 2014; Otto & Estrada, 2019). Validity of assessment can

DOI: 10.4324/9781003025115-5

be generally defined as whether the test score can accurately reflect a student's level of knowledge, skills, or competencies which the test is intended to measure (Hughes, 2003; Shaw & Imam, 2013). It is questionable whether assessment in EMI can accurately reflect students' levels of content knowledge because students are assessed through their L2, which is very often less proficient than their first language (L1). They may encounter language barriers when trying to express their understanding of the content knowledge and/or perform higher-order thinking skills in their L2 (Gablasova, 2014; Luk & Lin, 2015). When teachers interpret students' assessment results, they may not be able to diagnose whether students have mastered the content knowledge, or they may have difficulty in demonstrating their knowledge through their L2. In this sense, EMI assessments may not be valid. A related issue would be "fairness" of the assessment, especially in contexts where EMI students are compared with students who are learning the content subjects through their L1 (Shaw, 2012). While assessments should, in theory, be similar (or even the same) for both EMI and non-EMI students, teachers should also be aware that EMI students are not disadvantaged because of the language of instruction and assessment (Brinton et al., 2003).

The important role played by assessments is not only reflected by how they affect students' performance but also how they influence teachers' pedagogy, which is known as the backwash effect (Alderson & Wall, 1993). There have been more and more proposals calling teachers to provide more language scaffolding for students who are learning content knowledge through their L2 (e.g., An, Macaro, & Childs, 2019; Cammarata & Haley, 2018; Lo, Lin, & Cheung, 2018). Yet, when working with EMI teachers on professional development programmes and research on their classroom practices, we often observed that EMI teachers tended to prioritise content teaching and believe that language is not important. In Hong Kong, an examination-oriented context, it is exceptionally difficult to persuade EMI teachers to pay more attention to language, when teachers believe that as long as students could get the content accurate, they could still get the marks in assessments. In this sense, EMI teachers are not willing to spend more time on language in their lessons. This in turn undermines the effectiveness of any professional development programmes in EMI pedagogy. We gradually realised that perhaps one way to encourage teachers to modify their classroom practices is demonstrating the inseparable relationship between content and language and illustrating the fact that language plays a crucial role in students' performance in assessments.

It is against such background and personal conviction that I started this research project on assessment issues in bilingual education programmes such as EMI and content and language integrated learning (CLIL). Its major aim is to conduct a survey of the questions in EMI assessment so as to examine the interplay between content and language demands on students. Such a survey of questions was conducted through analysing a large sample of questions in EMI assessments. In other words, the research method employed was text analysis, which has been adopted in a couple of previous studies. For example, Shaw and Imam (2013) conducted text analysis of the examination papers and students' scripts in an internationally recognised examination (IGCSE) to identify the linguistic features and demands that various subjects (biology, geography, and history) imposed on candidates; Chan (2016) analysed junior secondary school internal examination papers in Hong Kong and categorised the questions into the various cognitive levels of Bloom's taxonomy. To a certain extent, my research project was similar to these previous studies. However, my project analysed the assessment questions in terms of the "interplay" between content and language demands, and it included a large number of questions extracted from different types of assessments (i.e., formative vs summative assessments) and different grade levels, which would then allow us to see the connection between instruction and assessment and to examine the progression across different stages of education.

This project was conducted in Hong Kong, where EMI has been practised in secondary schools for decades. With the most recent medium of instruction (MOI) policy implemented since 2010, secondary schools can decide on their own MOI (L1 Chinese or L2 English), according to students' ability, teachers' capacity, and schools' support measures. Owing to the general preference for EMI education (based on the assumption that it can facilitate English learning), many secondary schools in Hong Kong are teaching at least some content subjects through English (Kan, Lai, Kirkpatrick, & Law, 2011). Thus, in Hong Kong, students usually take six years of primary education using Chinese Medium Instruction (CMI), followed by six years of secondary education using either CMI or EMI across different subjects. Upon finishing secondary education, the grade 12 students (aged around 17) will take the Hong Kong Diploma of Secondary Education Examination (HKDSE), a standardised high-stakes university entrance exam in either Chinese or English, depending on their choice of MOI at schools. The contents in the Chinese and English versions of the HKDSE are the same. Given its long-lasting debate over MOI policy and exam-oriented culture in Hong Kong (Carless, 2011), Hong Kong provides a suitable context for this research on assessment issues in EMI.

5.2 Research planning

When it comes to text analysis of the questions, we could conduct qualitative or quantitative analysis, or a combination of both. In the studies reviewed earlier, Shaw and Iman (2013) analysed the language features of questions in different subjects by adopting a more qualitative, descriptive approach, whereas Chan (2016) coded the cognitive levels of the questions with reference to the six levels in Bloom's taxonomy and then summarised the findings with descriptive statistics. Considering our goal of providing an overview of questions in different types of assessments, and comparing the trends in different types of assessments and different grade levels, we decided to go for a more quantitative-oriented approach – each question extracted from EMI assessments would be coded according to the cognitive and language demands, and these codes would then be summarised to reveal the trends.

After making the decision to go for quantitative analysis, a follow-up decision would be the analytical or coding framework to be used. A few analytical frameworks proposed or used in previous studies had been considered, including the assessment matrix of "what" and "how" proposed by Short (1993) for the English Language Learners in the U.S., the Content and Language Integrated Learning Assessment (CLILA) model proposed by Massler et al. (2014), and the assessment grid consisting of the dimensions of cognitive demands and linguistic demands proposed by myself and Lin (2014). The framework proposed by Lo and Lin (2014) was chosen to form the basis of the coding process in this project, based on three major reasons. First, the framework was proposed and tried out in the Hong Kong EMI context, which was the same as the research context of the current project. Second, the framework is in the form of a matrix between cognitive and language demands, which fits the aims of this project to analyse the "interplay" between the two dimensions. Third, the framework depicts different levels of cognitive and language demands, which in turn allows an examination of the differences in different types of assessment and grade levels in terms of its level of difficulty or complexity. More pedagogical implications could be drawn from such a comparison (see Section 5.4.2 for the details of this framework). After having made these two important decisions, the design and scope of the project could be planned.

5.3 Research design

This research project is basically text analysis. It may avoid some research design issues concerning access to and recruitment of research participants and design of such research instruments as observation protocols, interview questions, and questionnaires. However, it was important to decide on the scope of study, data collection, and analysis procedures. The first decision to make was which subject(s) to include. There are over ten content subjects in the curriculum and it is important to decide how many and which subjects to focus on so that the data collected would be representative of the cognitive and language demands across different subjects and at the same time manageable by the research team. The project eventually decided to focus on two subjects, namely integrated science (junior secondary)/biology (senior secondary) and geography. The choice of these two subjects was justified by two reasons. First, it would be desirable to include one science and one humanities subject, as it has been observed that the linguistic demands involved in different subject disciplines vary (Lo, 2014; Shaw & Imam, 2013). Second, the two particular subjects are offered by over 90% of secondary schools in Hong Kong (Hong Kong Examinations and Assessment Authority [HKEAA], 2015a) and they can be found across different stages in the secondary school curriculum (including both junior and senior levels). Including these subjects would then enable the researchers to tap into the assessment experience of a large proportion of secondary school students, and to examine any changes across different grade levels.

Another aim of the project is to compare the questions in different types of assessments. But how to define these different "types" of assessments? For instance, there could be formative and summative assessments, internal and external assessments, low-stakes and high-stakes assessments, self-designed and standardised assessments, and so on. Comparing different "pairs" of assessments may yield different insights into assessment design and pedagogy. The research team finally went for "formative and summative assessments", as they have been widely discussed and researched in assessment and testing literature (e.g., Black & Wiliam, 1998; Carless, 2011) and, to a certain extent, formative and summative assessments encompass other types of assessments. For instance, formative assessments, which usually aim to collect information about students' performances so as to provide feedback for teaching and learning, may coincide with internal and low-stakes assessments; whereas summative assessments, which are conducted to evaluate students' levels of achievement at a given point in time, can be represented by high-stakes, standardised assessments. In our research project, formative assessments are represented by students' homework, whereas summative assessments are represented by the school-based examinations and the public university entrance examination.

After delineating the subjects and types of assessments, the question of how to sample the assessment questions followed. While it was straightforward to gather the questions in the public examinations (which are published every year after the examination), it was more complicated to collect questions from formative assessments and school-based examinations so that they were representative. For formative assessments, we decided to extract the questions from two sets of textbooks (together with their associated workbooks) which were the most popular among secondary schools in

Hong Kong. And for school-based examinations, we sent invitation emails to a stratified random sample of secondary schools and asked the teachers to share their examination papers. By doing so, we acknowledged the limitation of such a sampling method in that we assumed teachers and students largely relied on the textbooks and workbooks, and we excluded some supplementary questions designed by teachers. However, we believed that might be the most feasible way to sample a large number of assessment questions.

5.4 Method in detail

5.4.1 Data sources

The data of this study were mainly assessment questions in EMI and they came from three sources. First, questions were collected from a set of textbooks and the accompanying workbooks of science/biology and geography. The science and biology textbooks are used for the junior secondary and senior secondary curriculum, respectively. These sets of textbooks and workbooks were selected based on their popularity among local secondary schools, and they were written based on the curriculum guidelines stipulated by the Hong Kong Education Bureau. These textbooks represented formative assessments in schools. There were, altogether, 2,491 questions from junior form science, 1,940 questions from senior form biology, 1,386 questions from junior form geography, and 500 questions from senior form geography.

Second, the end-of-term/year examination papers set by science/biology and geography teachers in local secondary schools with EMI classes were gathered. These represented the school-based summative assessment practices designed by content subject teachers. Considering the time frame and human resources available, the examination papers were collected from ten secondary schools in Hong Kong, which were randomly sampled and invited from different districts in Hong Kong. This set of papers provided 767 science/biology and 807 geography questions.

Third, questions were extracted from the annually held HKDSE from 2012 (the first year when it was administered) to 2015 (the year before the project was carried out). As mentioned earlier, this high-stakes public examination is taken by students at grade 12 (aged around 17) prior to entering tertiary education. There were 387 biology and 354 geography questions from these sets of HKDSE papers.

With data coming from textbooks across junior and senior secondary levels, as well as school examination and public examination papers, our analysis could explore any differences between formative assessments (represented by textbooks and workbooks) and summative assessments (represented by the school examination and public examination papers), and the progression between different grade levels.

5.4.2 Data analysis

The assessment questions sampled and analysed totaled 8,632. Our unit of analysis was each question or each part of the multi-part assessment question. We considered this a more appropriate analysis because questions are sometimes broken down into several parts and each part might have a distinctive demand different from the other parts of the same question.

First, the cognitive and linguistic demands of each question or each part of the multi-part question were coded with the framework shown in Table 5.1 (Lo & Fung, 2020). This framework consists of two main dimensions. The first one is "cognitive demand", which can be divided into three levels, namely "recall", "application", and "analysis". These levels are condensed from the six levels in Bloom's taxonomy (Bloom, 1956; Krathwohl, 2002). Along the other dimension is "linguistic demand", which is further categorised into "productive" (involving writing and speaking) and "receptive" (requiring reading and listening). The three basic levels in the linguistic demand dimension are "vocabulary", "sentence patterns", and "text", which correspond to the various features of academic language identified (Lin, 2016; Schleppegrell, 2004). For "productive linguistic demand", one more level "no productive demand" was added, as some questions

Table 5.1 The analytical/coding framework adopted in the research project

Linguistic\cognitive demand		Recall	Application	Analysis
Receptive vocabulary	No productive demand			
	Productive vocabulary			
	Productive sentence			
	Productive text			
Receptive sentence	No productive demand			
	Productive vocabulary			
	Productive sentence			
	Productive text			
Receptive text	No productive demand			
	Productive vocabulary			
	Productive sentence			
	Productive text			

Source: Lo & Fung (2020)

(e.g., multiple-choice questions, graph plotting questions) do not require students to produce any language. Using this framework, each question was coded according to its cognitive and (productive and receptive) linguistic demands. For example, the following question appears in the HKDSE 2015 biology paper (HKEAA, 2015b, p. 30): "Although both arteries and veins are blood vessels, they are very different in their structure. Discuss how their structural differences are related to the different ways of maintaining blood flow inside the blood vessels." This question can be analysed as exerting a "receptive sentence" demand and a "productive text" demand because students need to read the questions presented in sentences and write an essay. At the same time, the question also imposes "analysis cognitive demand" because students are asked to use their higher-order thinking skills to compare and contrast arteries and veins as two different types of blood vessels.

The coding of assessment questions was conducted separately by a research team member. Inter-rater reliability was sought for around 15% of all data (1,264 questions), rendering a 94% agreement. All discrepancies were discussed and resolved by the coders. The coding results could reveal the distribution of the cognitive and linguistic demands of the questions found in different types of assessments. To examine whether there are any differences between junior secondary and senior secondary assessments, as well as between formative and summative assessments, chi-square tests were performed to compare the cognitive and linguistic demands of the questions from different sources (e.g., junior form textbooks against senior form textbooks; senior form textbooks against HKDSE papers).

At the beginning of the project, the research team planned to analyse the questions from two sets of textbooks and workbooks from each content subject so as to capture more questions students may encounter. However, after collecting one set of textbooks and workbooks, the research team realised that the number of assessment questions far exceeded their expectations. To strike a balance between the representativeness of data and the resources available, the research team decided to reduce the scope of data collection from including two sets of textbooks to one set of textbooks for each subject, which still generated over 6,000 questions.

While conducting the question analysis using the analytical framework, the research team found that the coding process involved some judgement. For example, the three levels of cognitive demands were condensed from the six levels of Bloom's taxonomy so as to make the framework simpler. However, the boundary between the three levels was not always clear-cut, and sometimes it may be difficult to determine whether a question requires "application" or "analysis". A similar issue was also found when analysing the linguistic demands, where it may be hard to judge whether a question is expecting production at the "sentence" or "text" level (e.g., how many sentences would become a text?). Another issue concerns the "inferred"

demands versus "actual" demands. When analysing the questions, the demands imposed or expected were actually the researchers' interpretation. This may be different from students' actual experience. For example, in the geography subject, one typical question looks like this: "Explain how (factor A) and (factor B) may lead to (a phenomenon)". As the question expects students to tease out the cause-effect relationship between a phenomenon and its factors, the researchers would normally code it as "application" in the cognitive dimension. However, it may be the case that students may have memorised the relevant explanation from the textbook and what they need to do to address the question is only "recall".

I would argue that these issues involved in using coding framework are common and, to a certain extent, inevitable. To resolve the issues and enhance the validity of the coding framework and reliability of our analysis, we did several things: first, we provided coding training for the research team members before the coding process; second, we encouraged frequent discussion whenever members were puzzled by the coding of some questions; third, we established inter-rater reliability by comparing the coding of two researchers of 15% of all the questions; fourth, we modified our original framework after some initial analyses, which would provide a more fine-grained and valid analysis of the questions (see more details about this revision process in the next section). Also, we did acknowledge the limitation of conducting this kind of text analysis, although we believed that the findings would serve as the first stage of future studies.

5.5 Practical lessons learned

We started this project with a view to providing an overview of the questions in assessment in EMI education so as to infer the demands imposed on students in both language and content dimensions. To generate a comprehensive picture, we decided to conduct text analysis of questions found in different types of assessment. With a coding framework, we coded over 8,500 questions, generated some descriptive statistics to reveal the trends, and conducted some inferential statistical tests to compare the patterns found in different types of assessment and across grade levels. To facilitate the analysis of such a large number of questions, it is crucial to be very cautious during the process of setting up the project and early stage of analysis. We have learned two important lessons.

The first one concerns the validity of the coding framework. A valid coding framework is essential for valid and reliable data analysis. Hence, it is important to validate the framework at the beginning of the project. Our process of validation consisted of two phases: (1) we constructed the framework based on previous theoretical literature (e.g., Bloom's taxonomy, characteristics of academic language), and (2) we validated and refined the framework through pilot study and early stage data collection. The second phase was particularly important, as theoretical literature may not always be applicable to actual data. In this project, we originally adopted the framework proposed by Lo and Lin (2014), which only consisted of three levels of cognitive demands and three levels of linguistic demands (i.e., vocabulary, sentence, and text). After applying this framework to the data collected for this study, we felt the need to revise the framework so as to analyse the data more accurately. First, the linguistic demand was separated into "receptive" and "productive" demands, since every question contains receptive linguistic information to decode, the level of which could be different from the productive language requirement. Second, the revised framework contains an additional level of "no productive linguistic demand", as we found that quite a number of questions (particularly multiple-choice questions) do not require any language production. In this way, the revised framework (shown in Table 5.1) could generate a more specific and fine-grained analysis of assessment questions. It has to be noted that any coding framework or taxonomy should be regarded as a starting point, and it is always subject to revision, based on reiterative processes of applying the framework to the data collected for a particular study.

The second lesson learned is related to containing subjectivity. Even though we have carefully constructed a coding framework, it does not mean that the data analysis process is straightforward. As previously mentioned, analysing the questions involved some personal judgement, especially when the boundaries between the different levels of cognitive and linguistic demands were not absolutely clear. To minimise subjectivity, we had training for researchers and established inter-rater reliability. During the process of coding, research team members also included some additional notes to explain how to differentiate the various levels, which would help align the coding of different researchers. For example, the research team constructed the following table (Table 5.2) to elaborate on the different levels of cognitive demands:

Table 5.2 Notes on classification of cognitive demands

Cognitive demands	Some criteria in classification	Typical question words or language structures
Recall	– Describe something factual – No new scenario presented – Even without understanding the specific scenario, one can answer the question	– Describe, give, state, name – What is . . . ?

Cognitive demands	Some criteria in classification	Typical question words or language structures
Apply	– Apply factual knowledge to a problem/new or specific scenario – Need explanation (i.e., recall theory and apply to this case) (requires reasoning) (NOT dependent on type of questions e.g., MC asking why something happens can also be *apply*)	– Explain the results, explain the graph, explain how/why something works/happens
Analyse	– Involve evaluation, comparison (with reasoning, e.g., describing or explaining differences), synthesis – Sometimes with a new scenario + modification of the scenario (e.g., first part of a question presents an experiment investigating transpiration rate of a plant, then in the second part, the researcher put a fan near it, and the question asks what might happen) – Sometimes involve some hypothetical elements/creation of an experiment/opinion on something	– Deduce, compare, contrast, evaluate – Suggest/comment on the advantage of something – What else might be done? – What conclusions can you draw from the experiment? – What are the possible consequences? – Explain the importance of something – Explain/state the difference (involves comparison) – although the language/ emphasis could be different

When analysing individual questions, researchers may also add some notes or remarks to explain the coding. For example, when analysing the cognitive demand of a question from the science textbook, the researcher remarked "Explain how the results provide support to the hypothesis: need to synthesise the information and justify the results" to justify the coding of "analysis"; for another question coded "recall", the researcher explained with this note "can find the answer from the text directly". With these measures, researchers' subjectivity could be contained, and the data analysis would not be affected even when there was turnover in research team members. Such an "audit trail", which usually documents all research decisions and activities (e.g., data collection chronology, record of data analysis procedures; Creswell & Miller, 2000), is common in qualitative research to ensure its credibility and trustworthiness. I would argue that such an audit trail is also useful in quantitative research.

5.6 Concluding summary

This research project aims to examine the current assessment practices of EMI education, particularly focusing on the interplay between cognitive and linguistic demands imposed on students. It also sought to compare the demands involved in different types of assessment and across different key learning stages. With systematic analysis of the questions gathered from different sources, the following trends were observed:

1   Regardless of grade levels and subjects, students are encountering both cognitive and linguistic demands in EMI assessments. Even at junior secondary levels, most questions require receptive language skills (i.e., reading and understanding the questions presented in sentences). Such linguistic demands appear to increase by grade level.
2   Regardless of subjects, there appears to be a progression in both cognitive and linguistic demands when students proceed to senior secondary levels. In particular, most questions at junior secondary ask for "recall" and "application" skills and require little language production, but those at senior secondary ask for "application" and "analytical" skills and require students to write sentences or short texts.
3   Comparing formative and summative assessments, it is observed that the cognitive and linguistic demands imposed by questions in textbooks/workbooks and those in school-based examinations are rather similar. However, the questions in the public examination, HKDSE, appear to be more cognitively and linguistically challenging than those in senior secondary textbooks/workbooks.

In addition to providing an overview of assessment practices in EMI, the data in this project in turn further validated the analytical framework (Table 5.1). Such a framework could be adopted in future studies to facilitate systematic analysis of questions in EMI assessment, which in turn helps determine how questions are distributed in different forms of assessment, guide the development of EMI assessment with enhanced validity, and inform EMI pedagogy, especially concerning whether teachers are providing enough support for students to tackle both cognitive and linguistic demands in assessment.

The method of text analysis could serve as the main purpose of this research project (i.e., to do a survey of EMI assessments). However, one challenge against such text analysis may be the fact that the cognitive and linguistic demands are "inferred" by the researchers, which may be different from those "experienced" by students. Hence, the text analysis could be accompanied by analysis of students' sample work and their real-time cognitive processes with, for example, interviews, think-aloud protocols, or stimulated recalls. The combination of different research methods will provide an even more comprehensive picture of the challenges encountered by students when tackling EMI assessments, and their coping strategies.

References

Alderson, J. C., & Wall, D. (1993). Does washback exist? *Applied Linguistics*, *14*(2), 115–129. doi:10.1093/applin/14.2.115

An, J., Macaro, E., & Childs, A. (2019). Language focused episodes by monolingual teachers in science English Medium Instruction lessons. *Journal of Immersion and Content-Based Language Education*, *7*(2), 166–191. doi:10.1075/jicb.18019.an

Black, P., & Wiliam, D. (1998). Assessment and classroom learning. *Assessment in Education: Principles, Policy & Practice*, *5*(1), 7–74. doi:10.1080/0969595980 050102

Bloom, B. S. (1956). *Taxonomy of educational objectives, Handbook I: The cognitive domain*. New York: David McKay Co Inc.

Brinton, D. M., Snow, M. A., & Wesche, M. B. (2003). *Content-based second language instruction*. Ann Arbor, MI: University of Michigan Press.

Cammarata, L., & Haley, C. (2018). Integrated content, language, and literacy instruction in a Canadian French immersion context: A professional development journey. *International Journal of Bilingual Education and Bilingualism*, *21*(3), 332–348. doi:10.1080/13670050.2017.1386617

Carless, D. (2011). *From testing to productive student learning: Implementing formative assessment in Confucian-heritage settings*. New York: Routledge.

Chan, J. Y. H. (2016). The fine-tuning medium-of-instruction policy in Hong Kong: A case study of the changing school-based test papers in Science subjects. *Education Journal*, *44*(1), 159–193.

Creswell, J. W., & Miller, D. L. (2000). Determining validity in qualitative inquiry. *Theory into Practice*, *39*(3), 124–130. doi:10.1207/s15430421tip3903_2

Gablasova, D. (2014). Issues in the assessment of bilingually educated students: Expressing subject knowledge through L1 and L2. *The Language Learning Journal*, *42*(2), 151–164. doi:10.1080/09571736.2014.891396

HKEAA (Hong Kong Examinations and Assessment Authority). (2015a). *2015 HKDSE entry statistics*. Retrieved from www.hkeaa.edu.hk/DocLibrary/HKDSE/ Exam_Report/Examination_Statistics/dseexamstat15_2.pdf

HKEAA (Hong Kong Examinations and Assessment Authority). (2015b). *HKDSE biology 2015 examination report and question papers*. Hong Kong: HKEAA.

Hughes, A. (2003). *Testing for language teachers* (2nd ed.). Cambridge, UK: Cambridge University Press.

Kan, V., Lai, K. C., Kirkpatrick, A., & Law, A. (2011). *Fine-tuning Hong Kong's medium of instruction policy*. Hong Kong: The Hong Kong Institute of Education.

Krathwohl, D. R. (2002). A revision of Bloom's taxonomy: An overview. *Theory into Practice*, *41*(4), 212–218. doi:10.1207/s15430421tip4104_2

Lin, A. M. Y. (2014). Critical discourse analysis in applied linguistics: A methodological review. *Annual Review of Applied Linguistics*, *34*, 213–232.

Lin, A. M. Y. (2016). *Language across the curriculum and CLIL in English-as-an-additional-language contexts: Theory and practice*. Dordrecht: Springer.

Lo, Y. Y. (2014). L2 language learning opportunities in different academic subjects in content-based instruction – evidence in favour of "conventional wisdom". *Language and Education*, *28*(2), 141–160. doi:10.1080/09500782.2013.786086

Lo, Y. Y., & Fung, D. (2020). Assessment in CLIL: The interplay of cognitive and linguistic demands and their progression in secondary education. *International Journal of Bilingual Education and Bilingualism, 23*(10), 1192–1210. doi:10.10 80/13670050.2018.1436519

Lo, Y. Y., & Lin, A. M. Y. (2014). Designing assessment tasks with language awareness: Balancing cognitive and linguistic demands. *Assessment and Learning, 3,* 97–119.

Lo, Y. Y., Lin, A. M. Y., & Cheung, T. C. L. (2018). Supporting EFL Learners' science literacy development in CLIL: A genre-based approach. In K. S. Tang & K. Danielsson (Eds.), *Global developments in literacy research for science education* (pp. 79–95). Singapore: Springer.

Luk, J., & Lin, A. M. Y. (2015). Voices without words: Doing critical literate talk in English as a second language. *TESOL Quarterly, 49*(1), 67–91. doi:10.1002/ tesq.161

Massler, U., Stotz, D., & Queisser, C. (2014). Assessment instruments for primary CLIL: The conceptualisation and evaluation of test tasks. *The Language Learning Journal, 42*(2), 137–150. doi:10.1080/09571736.2014.891371

Otto, A., & Estrada, J. L. (2019). Towards an understanding of CLIL assessment practices in a European context: Main assessment tools and the role of language in content subjects. *CLIL. Journal of Innovation and Research in Plurilingual and Pluricultural Education, 2*(1), 31–42.

Schleppegrell, M. (2004). *The language of schooling: A functional linguistics perspective*. New York: Routledge.

Shaw, S. (2012). International assessment of Geography through the medium of English: Analysing the language skills required. In P. Charzyński, K. Donert, & Z. Podgórski (Eds.), *Bilingual teaching – globalization, regional Geography and English integration* (pp. 24–44). Toruń, Poland: Association of Polish Adult Educators.

Shaw, S., & Imam, H. (2013). Assessment of international students through the medium of English: Ensuring validity and fairness in content-based examinations. *Language Assessment Quarterly, 10*(4), 452–475. doi:10.1080/15434303 .2013.866117

Short, D. J. (1993). Assessing integrated language and content instruction. *TESOL Quarterly, 27*(4), 627–656. doi:10.2307/3587399

6 Establishing quality criteria and an EMI certification procedure

Gregg Dubow, Susanne Gundermann, and Louise Northover

Abstract

While students are usually required to prove their English language competencies (typically at the C1 level based on the Common European Framework of Reference for Languages [CEFR]) in order to be admitted into an English Medium Instruction (EMI) course of study, it has been widely assumed by universities that teachers inherently possess the necessary language skills to teach in these settings. To our knowledge, only a few systematic measures have been taken to certify the speaking proficiency of teachers in EMI degree programmes in Europe. These measures assessed the oral skills of EMI teachers in testing settings. Yet the most vital stakeholders, the students, were absent from these assessments. Consequently, crucial communicative competencies for teaching with a multilingual, multicultural student body were not certified. Research in EMI has shown, however, that teacher competencies such as student-oriented teaching, intercultural transparency, and accommodation strategies for English as a lingua franca are cited by students as helpful in facilitating their content learning through English. Drawing on these insights along with elements from a communicative competence model and threshold descriptors from the CEFR, the EMI team from the Language Teaching Centre at the University of Freiburg has developed EMI-specific assessment criteria. These criteria expand on perceived gaps in the aforementioned quality assurance measures monitoring the quality of the teaching staff's language use in English-taught programmes. This chapter outlines these EMI-specific criteria and gives insight into their application based on quantitative and qualitative data from the assessment practice, with an outlook into implications for EMI practitioners.

Keywords: EMI assessment criteria, certification, quality assurance, language competencies, teacher assessment

DOI: 10.4324/9781003025115-6

6.1 EMI teacher assessment – initial idea for a certification procedure

While English-taught degree programmes usually specify language require-ments for prospective students, teachers rarely need to prove that they pos-sess language competencies equal or superior to those demanded of their students. This presumed proficiency demonstrates a great leap of faith when considering that EMI teachers have varying experience teaching their disci-pline in a foreign language, some having never taught in English.

Research shows that limited systematic efforts have been made to certify the English language skills of those teaching or planning to teach in the EMI classroom in higher education. Delft University of Technology carried out extensive testing – online tests and a 30-minute, four-part oral test using CEFR can-do statements – to ensure teachers had an oral proficiency at the C1 level of the Common European Framework of Reference for Languages (CEFR) or better (Klaassen & Bos, 2017). Likewise, the University of Copenhagen has developed an in-house assessment, named the Test of Oral English Profi-ciency for Academic Staff (TOEPAS). The TOEPAS assessment uses tailored criteria to assess teachers' language ability, whereby lecturers simulate lectur-ing and student interaction in groups of three (Kling & Dimova, 2015, 2018).

While both of these systematic schemes certify EMI teachers' English language skills, neither of them includes students' perspectives on their teachers' language use. In order to address this gap and embed student per-spectives into ensuring quality in EMI programmes, the EMI team from the Language Teaching Centre at the University of Freiburg designed, piloted, and applied EMI-specific criteria in actual English-taught lessons to assure quality in English-taught degree programmes. This chapter describes the conceptual framework for these EMI assessment criteria, outlines the certi-fication procedure and its ten criteria, and reflects on their application based on quantitative and qualitative data from the procedure. It concludes with a review of implications for EMI practitioners.

6.2 EMI quality assurance – how to measure and assess quality

In the initial planning phase, it was decided that English-taught content lessons would be observed and student feedback in the assessment of EMI teachers would be included. Embedding these two elements into the certification frame-work was paramount as the former allowed for an authentic snapshot of teach-ing, while the latter provided teachers with feedback from students – the most important stakeholders in the EMI equation. Thus, it was required to develop criteria which both assessors and students could rate and comment on.

To begin, potential assessment criteria were sketched by consulting a range of spoken production categories and C1 threshold descriptors from the CEFR as well as the International English Language Testing System (IELTS) speaking band descriptors. In particular, the CEFR is viewed as an adaptable testing framework for specific needs and contexts (Davidson & Fulcher, 2007). However, the EMI team's experience up to that point, based on dozens of classroom observations and feedback discussions with teachers, indicated that the CEFR descriptors geared towards native speaker standards are misguided for a linguistically rich EMI context largely comprised of second (and third) language users of English. This view is supported by Pilkinton-Pihko (2013), whose work on defining EMI assessment criteria casts doubt on the appropriateness of the CEFR assessment criteria and their tendency to juxtapose the assessment of second language users against native speaker standards.

Thus, the EMI team drew upon specific elements from four competency categories of a communicative competence model conceived for pedagogic use in language teaching (Celce-Murcia, Dornyei, & Thurrell, 1995). These categories covered linguistic competencies (phonology, syntax, and lexicon), discourse competencies (lecturing and interacting with students), sociocultural competencies (cross-cultural awareness, stylistic appropriateness, and paralinguistic factors), and strategic competencies (compensating lexical gaps and interactional strategies to negotiate clarification).

To sharpen this conceptual framework, the EMI team consulted studies on teachers' use of English as a Lingua Franca (ELF) and students' perceptions of ELF use. Pilkinton-Pihko (2013) has reported on teachers aiming for accessible fluency and intelligible pronunciation in their teaching instead of native speaker norms of fluency and accent-free pronunciation, while Björkman (2011) has noted that pragmatic strategies such as commenting on terms and signalling discourse structure are lesson features likely to increase opportunities for interaction and consequently student comprehension of lectures. With regard to learner perceptions, students have reported that the ability to explain supersedes language proficiency (Smit, 2010) and that reduced lecturing and more question opportunities are more vital than accurate language use based on native speaker norms (Gundermann, 2014).

After having synthesised these findings with the communicative competence model, the criteria were piloted in seven English-taught courses by two EMI assessors and students via questionnaires. Upon feedback from the observed teachers and an analysis of the results, standards for certified teaching performance were set. Ten EMI-specific criteria were forged and divided into two categories, linguistic and communicative competencies, and the wording of the criteria and student questionnaire items were

fine-tuned to strengthen explicitness. While the linguistic category criteria contain some references to target language standards, they essentially aim to ensure that the language skills proper of a non-native English speaker teacher are accessible and intelligible for students with varying language backgrounds. Conversely, the communicative category criteria make no references to target language standards and instead focus on a teacher's language use for didactic purposes in an EMI context. Dividing the criteria into these categories provides a more nuanced feedback of a teacher's strengths and weaknesses in English-taught lessons. In other words, a teacher may speak excellent English but lack in pragmatic strategies to support the non-native speaker learner, or a teacher may occasionally speak in less than intelligible or accessible terms but demonstrate solid didactic and communication strategies to interact with students. Before delving into the ten criteria, the next section lays out the broader certification procedure and how the marks are calculated.

6.3 Developing a certification procedure and assessment criteria

6.3.1 The certification procedure and evaluation process

While the intrinsic motivation for teachers to have an English-taught lesson evaluated lies in receiving individual feedback, extra motivation to participate was generated by offering the to certify the entire EMI degree programme. If at least 80% of the teaching staff is certified, the programme obtains a quality seal (see Figure 6.1) and a certificate attesting to the

Figure 6.1 The EMI^{QM} quality seal, attesting to certified competencies for English Medium Instruction

compensatory strategies to navigate lexical gaps/lapses (e.g., ". . . and then we find uhm . . . [searching for the adjective herbivorous] . . . animals which only eat plants"). Moreover, any instances of opaque idiomaticity are documented to raise awareness about how culturally specific metaphors or colloquialisms can exclude some students. For example, a teacher referring to a "filibuster" (a political tactic in American Congress) is likely to exclude students unfamiliar with such a culture specific term. Students indicate to what extent they were familiar with the words and expressions used by the lecturer.

Code consistency (L-5)

This criterion is divided into two sub-criteria. The first addresses the importance of only using English in both speech and writing in the EMI classroom. If content on slides or specific terms from another language are not briefly translated or explained in English, this can exclude students with little or no skills in the local language and become a source of frustration (Gundermann, 2014). This criterion does not negatively rate codeswitching provided the teacher follows up in English. This follow-up explanation or translation in English is the second point of focus for this criterion, that is, did a follow-up explanation or translation occur? Students are asked whether English was the only language used and, if not, whether a follow-up explanation or translation in English was given.

6.3.3 *The criteria for communicative competencies*

Cohesion (C-1)

This criterion highlights three sub-criteria of cohesion. First, on the macro-level, we document how explicitly teachers communicate the lesson introduction, consisting of an outline, learning objectives, and context (Thompson, 1994), since these features of lesson structure improve student retention (Bligh, 2000). Second, on the micro-level, we document the teachers' explicit use of signposts to transition, focus students' attention, communicate connections between lessons, and highlight key points. All these features have been identified as helpful pragmatic strategies in EMI contexts (Björkman, 2011) to help crystallise the teacher's line of thought and ease students' cognitive load. The final element focuses on lesson pace by pointing out the information density and the number of explicit question opportunities for students and deliberate transitions since both points make a lesson more accessible. Students indicate to what extent the lesson structure and learning objectives were clear and to what extent they were able to follow the lesson pace.

Prosody (C-2)

This communicative competency criterion is divided into two sub-criteria. First we assess para-verbal features (e.g., *intonation* or *speech rate*) as these can impact student comprehension. In particular, a quick speech rate can be tiresome to students and inhibit comprehension. To this end, students indicate to what extent they were able to follow the lecturer's speech rate. In addition, we comment on instances when teachers stress particular words or deliberately pause since these para-verbal skills help students to better absorb key ideas and focus their attention.

Initiation and integration of student input (C-3)

Posing questions or facilitating classroom exercises are vital to foster student input. In fact, students have self-reported better comprehension in EMI courses with more interaction (Suviniitty, 2012). Thus, this criterion is split into two sub-criteria. The first is used to document instances of initiating interaction, evaluate questions and classroom tasks for clarity and explicitness, and assess whether teachers allow students ample time to formulate answers. Students indicate to what extent they were involved in the lesson via either teacher questions or opportunities to ask questions. The second part of this criterion is to assess how teachers integrate student input. Teachers can act as conduits to ensure that student input is heard by the entire room to embed it into ongoing discourse and to utilize that input for further interaction and to involve other students. To this end, students indicate to what extent they linguistically understood their peers' contributions.

Responding to student input (C-4)

This criterion, split into two sub-criteria, concentrates on teachers responding to student input. We specifically focus on constructiveness and explicitness. More specifically, we comment on whether the teacher provides explicit feedback – beyond one-word responses – and, when possible, on whether the teacher offers follow-up questions for students to further engage with the content. Second, if instances of clarification arise, we comment on whether teachers navigate comprehension difficulties in a sociolinguistically appropriate manner – beyond, for example, "excuse me?" or "what?" – and whether they attempt to co-negotiate meaning by offering students opportunities to reformulate or clarify their original input. Students indicate to what degree they understood the lecturer's responses to student questions and contributions.

Intercultural transparency (C-5)

This criterion focuses on the importance of a teacher contextualising content-related examples. EMI teachers need to be transparent and contextualise references to local concepts (domestic institutes, geography, or national politics) in an international classroom so that students new to the local learning environment are not excluded (Gundermann, 2014). Students are asked whether references to local concepts/examples were made and if so, to what degree the lecturer contextualised these for the international students.

The next section provides an example of one criterion being applied from a dual perspective.

6.4 An excerpt of dual-perspective assessment criteria in practice

The following two tables show excerpts of qualitative feedback for the linguistic competency criterion *L-4 – Lexical range and accuracy* from a 90-minute lesson in an engineering course with 32 students. EMI assessors evaluate sub-descriptors for this criterion on a four-point scale and substantiate the mark with detailed documentation (Table 6.1). Students answer one item on a similar scale, albeit with adapted perspective. In addition, students can comment on what particularly helped them and what would have enabled them to better follow the lesson (Table 6.2).

In this lesson, several students viewed the examples used by the lecturer as helpful in demonstrating the importance and practicality of the topic covered. While the teacher's know-how and experiences are paramount for including such examples, it is also the teacher's ability to communicate these via lexical range and accuracy that help 'produce' this valued insight into the field. One student also noted "fundamental description in an easy way" as a helpful feature of the lesson, an observation that adds to the argument of the need for language to be accessible.

The detailed EMI assessor feedback documents lexical strengths and weaknesses, especially those which can disrupt comprehension. Of the two underlined errors in Table 6.1, the first one stems from first language interference ("share" is falsely translated for this context from the German word "*teilen*") while the second error is inaccurate ("divide" has a different meaning than the intended message of "differentiate" or "distinguish"). The excerpt of qualitative feedback shown in Table 6.2 demonstrates that despite occasional inaccurate word choice, 90.6% of the students indicated they were familiar with the teacher's lexicon and even praised an element of the lesson partially dependent on lexical range and accuracy.

Table 6.1 Excerpt of EMI assessors' feedback on the linguistic criterion lexical range and accuracy (L-4)

Descriptor	Scale[1]				Assessors' documentation
	1	*2*	*3*	*4*	
Lexical choice was accurate according to target-language standards.	X[2]	X			**Examples of accurate lexical choice within context:** Financial basis for, objects are blurred, govern the formation of a process, collect and balance data **Inaccurate lexical choice which doesn't disrupt comprehension:** Solution is makeable, further or later, discriminate two types of clients **Inaccurate lexical choice which can disrupt comprehension:** (24:39–24:44)[3] "We have to a bit *share and divide* characteristic and function" (teacher meant categorise and differentiate between)
Lexical range was broad enough to elaborate on subject-specific content and manage classroom activities.	X	X			**Describing a content-related example:** (37:58–38:11) "Usually in this blood pressure monitor you have a cuff that is put above around your arm and then you inflate the cuff then slowly deflate it and then you measure the systolic and diastolic onset of pulsations". (24:31–24:38) "This is a characteristic and this is the first point where I want to guide you. A function is one thing; a characteristic that describes a function is another thing".

Note: This table shows merged feedback from two assessors (n = 2).
1 The scale (1–4) is worded in the assessor evaluation sheets as follows: consistently (1), to a large extent (2), to a moderate extent (3), to a small extent (4).
2 The X shows each assessor's mark given.
3 The time references in brackets refer to the video-recording of the lesson.

The following two tables show an excerpt of qualitative feedback for the communicative competency criterion *C-1 – Cohesion* from the same lesson.

It was particularly surprising that the majority of the students in this observed lesson (81.3%) agreed that the structure and learning objectives of the lesson were clearly communicated, although EMI assessor feedback documented that both points could have been more explicit. This discrepancy may indicate that students identify structure through other aspects of the course (homework assignments, course syllabus) or that learning objectives have been communicated through other mediums unknown to EMI assessors at the time of observation.

Table 6.2 Excerpt of student feedback on the linguistic criterion lexical range and accuracy (L-4)

Questionnaire item	Scale[1]				Student comments (what helped them better understand the lesson)
	1	*2*	*3*	*4*	
I was familiar with the words and expressions used by the lecturer.	90.6%[2]	9.4%	0%	0%	– examples – good practical examples – fundamental description in an easy way – lecturer uses very good examples

Note: This table shows merged feedback from the 32 students who attended this lesson (n = 32).
1 The scale (1–4) is worded in the student feedback questionnaires as follows: I agree (1), I tend to agree (2), I tend to disagree (3), I disagree (4).
2 The values show the percentage of students who gave each mark.

6.5 Findings, lessons learned, and potential implications

The certification procedure was applied to 87 courses in five different English-taught programmes with 1,678 student questionnaires completed during a period of six semesters. Marks generated from both EMI assessor evaluation and student feedback on these criteria resulted in 85 teachers having their linguistic and communicative competencies to teach in English certified. The graphs below show the combined dual-perspective results of the five certified English-taught programmes in 87 courses. Some preliminary conclusions on their application can be drawn.

With (Figure 6.2), EMI assessors and students marked teachers high and rarely indicated language barriers. While minimal pronunciation issues – due to first-language interference from German – were observed, the majority of students responded that no extra effort was required to understand the lecturer's pronunciation and that their comprehension of the lesson was not inhibited.

Concerning lexical repertoire, students often cited the use of examples as a helpful element. Figure 6.3 shows the five most frequent answers to the open-ended question "What helped me understand the lesson?" from the student questionnaire. Out of the 724 responses given in total, "examples" was stated 165 times (23% of all answers). The use of examples not only eases student comprehension but also indicates the teacher's ability to explain complex topics in accessible language. On this note, "giving explanations" was mentioned 99 times (13% of all answers). The fourth most mentioned element is "interaction" (mentioned 86 times, 12% of all answers). Classroom interaction is fundamental for any group size and lesson format. Student-oriented teaching, compared to teacher-centred lectures, not only helps

Table 6.3 Excerpt of EMI assessors' feedback on the communicative criterion cohesion (C-1)

Descriptor	Scale[1]				Assessors' documentation
	1	2	3	4	
Lecturer clearly expressed the structure and learning objectives of the lesson.		XX[2]			(1:06–1:40)[3] Clearly communicated where today's lesson relates to previous lessons on the design process The **learning objectives** could be more explicitly formulated (1:40–1:58) "Now we are about to set up the requirements. So what is the function of this product and how do I give this function numbers? And it is setting up this specification that we practice today?" No explicit outline for this particular lesson was given.
Lecturer used a range of cohesive devices to structure the lesson.	X	X			**Signpost for transitioning:** (8:55) "Let's go into detail what this means" **Signpost to connect dots within lesson/course:** (42:40) "You will do for the next two and a half weeks this task to write a specification sheet for a product".
Lesson pace was appropriate (rate of introducing content, opportunities to ask questions).	XX				There was a mix of lecturing and questions to vary pace and allow students to comment on content.

Note: This table shows merged feedback from two assessors (n = 2).
1 The scale (1–4) is worded in the assessor evaluation sheets as follows: consistently (1), to a large extent (2), to a moderate extent (3), to a small extent (4).
2 The X shows each assessor's mark given.
3 The time references in brackets refer to the video-recording of the lesson.

students learn more efficiently but also allows the teacher to check student comprehension, which is vital for a multilingual, multicultural student body. Moreover, student contributions are not always linguistically clear to the other students, as students are not necessarily familiar with each other's accents and acoustics can hinder comprehension. Therefore, teachers need to act as conduits by integrating multilingual groups of students and facilitating further interaction at all times.

Table 6.4 Excerpt of student feedback on the communicative criterion cohesion (C-1)

Questionnaire item	Scale[1]				Student comments (what helped them better understand the lesson)
	1	*2*	*3*	*4*	
The structure and learning objectives of today's lesson were clear.	81.3%[2]	18.8%	0%	0%	
I was able to follow the lesson pace (speed of introducing new information).	78.1%	21.9%	0%	0%	
The lecturer gave us sufficient opportunities to ask questions and/or make comments.	81.8%	15.2%	3%	0%	Questions and answers

Note: This table shows merged feedback from the 32 students who attended this lesson (n = 32).
1 The scale (1–4) is worded in the student feedback questionnaires as follows: I agree (1), I tend to agree (2), I tend to disagree (3), I disagree (4).
2 The values show the percentage of students who gave each mark.

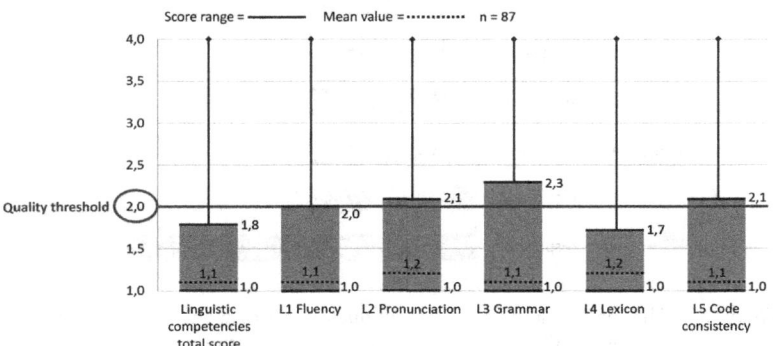

Figure 6.2 Aggregate dual-perspective results of linguistic competencies in 87 lessons of the five certified English-taught programmes

Note: Each bar represents the score range for the respective criterion and the dotted line illustrates the mean score for that competency.

Figure 6.4 shows the five most frequent answers to the open-ended question "What would help me better follow the lesson?" from the student questionnaire. Out of the 278 responses given to this question, "examples" was the answer given the most (stated 42 times; 15% of all answers) further emphasising that the use of examples eases student comprehension.

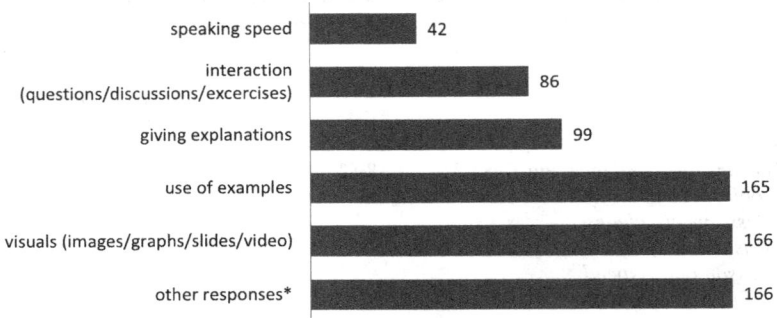

Figure 6.3 The top five aggregate student questionnaire answers to the open-ended question "What helped me understand the lesson?"

Note: In total 724 responses were given. Data was collected in 87 lessons in five different English-taught programmes; 1,678 student questionnaires were completed during a period of six semesters.

* Other responses referred to lesson pace, loud and clear voice, high level of English, lesson structure, given comparisons, repetition, and pre-lesson material.

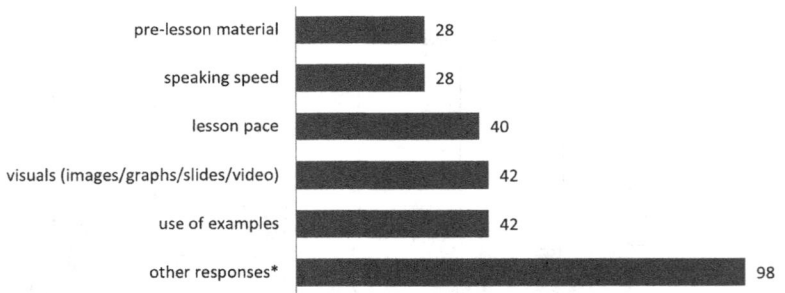

Figure 6.4 The top five aggregate student questionnaire answers to the open-ended question "What would help me better follow the lesson?"

Note: In total 278 responses were given to this question. Data was collected in 87 lessons in five different English-taught programmes; 1,678 student questionnaires were completed during a period of six semesters.

* Other responses referred to giving explanations/definitions, pronunciation, repetition, loud voice, interaction (questions/discussions/exercises), intonation, clear structure, and peers speaking clearly.

A suitable "lesson pace" (stated 40 times; 15% of all answers), an appropriate "speaking speed" (stated 28 times; 10% of all answers), and receiving pre-lesson material (stated 28 times; 10% of all answers) are three factors stressed as important to follow lesson content. Already being familiar with lesson content (concepts, lexical, etc.) and the pace of introducing new content are vital to ease student comprehension in an EMI classroom.

Regarding communicative competencies (Figure 6.5), EMI assessors and students marked teachers lower than on their linguistic competencies and often commented on specific features of the lesson. In particular, structure and speech rate were often cited by students with the former being substantiated in part by EMI assessor documentation of clear signposts to signal transitions, focus attention, and communicate connections. Regarding interaction, though, frequency and form differed. EMI assessors usually observed teacher questions to be, for the most part, linguistically clear and explicit enough. When teachers posed questions, other aspects of communicative competencies arose such as teachers giving students enough time to formulate "good" answers in a foreign language and repeating student responses for the entire room to understand.

Two contradictions were repeatedly observed in the application of the dual-perspective criteria. Although teachers often failed to state explicit learning objectives at the beginning of observed lessons, students rarely commented on or evaluated this negatively despite it being a questionnaire item. First, perceptions of intercultural transparency proved puzzling at times as students reported references to locally specific concepts in some lessons although none were observed or perceived by EMI assessors. In some cases, students marked the lesson low on this criterion despite no observed instances of intercultural murkiness. Could students be answering the question with other aspects of the course in mind and not exclusively on the one observed lesson as they were requested to do? Researching student

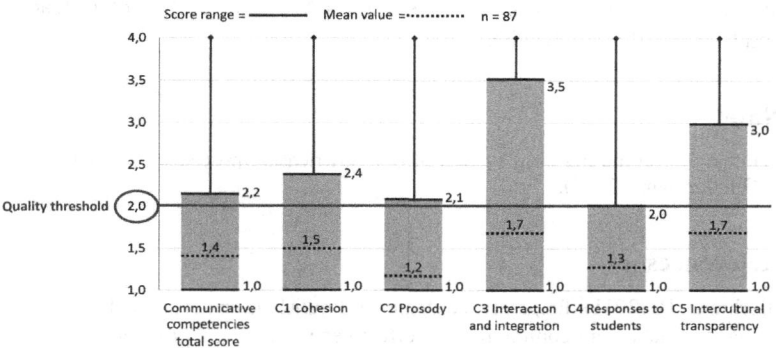

Figure 6.5 Aggregate dual-perspective results of communicative competencies in 87 lessons of the five certified English-taught programmes

Note: Each bar represents the score range for the respective criterion and the dotted line illustrates the mean score for that competency.

interpretations and views via focus group and stimulated recall interviews are required to deeper probe student perceptions.

On a broader note, it proved difficult or impossible to evaluate intercultural transparency based on one classroom observation. In hindsight, this criterion should be omitted as a mark contributing criterion and instead be a qualitative point to address (open-ended question). Regarding linguistic competencies, it is debatable whether fluency, grammar, and code consistency should be mark-contributing criteria. The EMI team's experience showed that teachers are fluent speakers with good command of grammar thanks to their extensive experience abroad as students, academics, and/or professionals in their respective fields. Marks for these criteria positively skewed overall results and could thus mask deficits on the communicative/didactic side of language use for the EMI context. Looking back on the certified teachers and programmes, five criteria were of importance in evaluating the quality of English-taught courses: pronunciation and articulation, lexical accuracy and range, cohesion, initiation and integration of student input, and responding to student input. For future assessment schemes, practitioners can assume the linguistic competencies and focus on criteria addressing communication and didactic skills for a linguistically and culturally heterogeneous student body at the tertiary level.

The dual-perspective assessment criteria have created a broad snapshot of English-taught courses in one German context. The picture shows lessons taught with minimally perceived language barriers. Students frequently commented on the positive and/or negative impact interaction, lesson pace, speech rate, explanations, and examples had on their learning; this feedback can be interpreted as students attributing more importance to didactic competencies than to language proficiency. We view this conclusion as a paramount implication for practitioners in the EMI field (both content teachers and trainers of those teachers).

Note

1 For more on the marking system of our certification procedure, see Dubow and Gundermann (2017).

References

Björkman, B. (2011). Pragmatic strategies in English as an academic lingua franca: Ways of achieving communicative effectiveness? *Journal of Pragmatics, 43*(4), 950–964. doi:10.1016/j.pragma.2010.07.033

Bligh, D. A. (2000). *What's the use of lectures?* San Francisco: Jossey-Bass.

Celce-Murcia, M., Dörnyei, Z., & Thurrell, S. (1995). Communicative competence: A pedagogically motivated model with content specifications. *Issues in Applied Linguistics, 6*(2), 5–35. Retrieved from http://escholarship.org/uc/item/2928w4zj

Common European Framework of Reference (CEFR). (2001). *CEFR – Common European framework of reference for languages*. Retrieved from www.coe.int/en/web/common-european-framework-reference-languages

Crystal, D. (2008). *A dictionary of linguistics and phonetics* (6th ed.). Oxford: Blackwell Publishing.

Dubow, G., & Gundermann, S. (2017). Certifying the linguistic and communicative competencies of teachers in English-medium instruction programmes. *Language Learning in Higher Education, 7*(2), 475–487. doi:10.1515/cercles-2017-0021

Gundermann, S. (2014). *English-medium instruction: Modelling the role of the native speaker in a Lingua Franca context* (Doctoral dissertation). University of Freiburg. doi:10.6094/978-3-928969-55-0

Klaassen, R. G., & Bos, M. (2017). English language screening for scientific staff at Delft University of Technology. *HERMES – Journal of Language and Communication in Business, 23*(45), 61–75. doi:10.7146/hjlcb.v23i45.97347

Kling, J., & Dimova, S. (2015). The test of oral English for academic staff (TOEPAS): Validation of standards and scoring procedures. In A. Knapp & K. Aguado (Eds.), *Fremdsprachen in Studium und Lehre – Chancen und Herausforderungen für den Wissenserwerb (Foreign Languages in Higher Education)* (pp. 247–268). Frankfurt: Peter Language International Academic Publishers.

Kling, J., & Dimova, S. (2018). Assessing English-medium instruction lecturer language proficiency across disciplines. *TESOL Quarterly, 52*(3), 634–656. doi:10.1002/tesq.454

Pilkinton-Pihko, D. (2013). *English-medium instruction: Seeking assessment criteria for spoken professional English* (Doctoral dissertation). University of Helsinki. Retrieved from http://urn.fi/URN:ISBN:978-952-10-9520-7

Smit, U. (2010). *English as a lingua franca in higher education: A longitudinal study of classroom discourse*. Berlin: Walter de Gruyter.

Suviniitty, J. (2012). *Lecturers in English as a Lingua Franca: Interactional Features* (Doctoral dissertation). University of Helsinki. Retrieved from http://urn.fi/URN:ISBN:978-952-10-8540-6

Thompson, S. (1994). Frameworks and contexts: A genre-based approach to analysing lecture introductions. *English for Specific Purposes, 13*(2), 171–186. doi:10.1016/0889-4906(94)90014-0

7 Corpus linguistic methods in EMI research

A missed opportunity?

Reka R. Jablonkai

Abstract

Although corpus linguistic methods are widely used in analysing educational and professional discourse, there are surprisingly few studies that apply this approach to analyse discourse in EMI educational contexts. This chapter argues that in order to extend our understanding of EMI language use and the linguistic demand on students and teachers in EMI contexts, more studies are needed that exploit the potentials of corpora and corpus linguistic methods in EMI research. The chapter highlights three broad areas where EMI research could especially benefit from the use of corpus linguistic methods. First, the strengths of corpus linguistic methods are probably most obvious in investigating vocabulary and grammatical aspects of discourse, for example, vocabulary load and lexical and syntactic complexity of texts. Second, EMI studies that aim to explore specific contextual and disciplinary language variations can profit from corpus-based analytical frameworks such as multidimensional analysis that can provide comprehensive descriptions of such varieties. Finally, corpus-based studies can be applied to investigate interaction and discourse functions in texts. For such purposes corpus approaches are often used to identify features that emerge from the corpus as frequent words and lexical bundles for further analysis. Studies focusing on these aspects typically use corpus linguistic methods in combination with qualitative methods such as conversational analysis or investigate the recurring patterns qualitatively in concordance lines. The chapter reviewed the handful of studies that analysed corpora of classroom discourse and academic disciplinary discourses in EMI contexts and proposes further directions of corpus research in EMI to unlock its hitherto untapped potential.

Keywords: corpus-based methods, vocabulary load, EMI corpus, linguistic complexity, lexical bundles

DOI: 10.4324/9781003025115-7

7.1 Introduction

EMI researchers have called for studies that extend our understanding of EMI classroom discourse and the role of language in EMI in general (Dalton-Puffer & Smit, 2013; Macaro, 2019). Macaro (2019) argues that the role of language is very complex in EMI contexts. He identified several language issues relating to EMI including the use of L1, the importance of identifying highly frequent subject-specific words for certain subjects, and the context and discipline-specific nature of language use. Dalton-Puffer and Smit (2013) highlight the relevance of investigating classroom discourse especially in terms of the language functions (e.g., defining, hypothesising, predicting, or explaining) that help EMI teachers and students to achieve their communicative goals in the teaching and learning process. They also acknowledged that such language and discourse functions may vary according to the subject of interest, the mode of communication (e.g., spoken, written) and the speaker's role (teacher, student). Furthermore, a widely discussed language-related issue in EMI literature is whether and to what extent EMI contributes to English language learning and improvement (Macaro, Curle, Pun, An, & Dearden, 2018). Overall, the following language-related issues were suggested to be relevant for future EMI research (Dalton-Puffer & Smit, 2013; Macaro, 2019; Macaro et al., 2018):

- Context- and discipline-specific language use in EMI contexts
- Discipline and subject-specific learning outcomes in terms of language use and discipline-specific communicative competence required from students
- Heterogeneity of EMI students in terms of their English proficiency in general and their knowledge of vocabulary in particular
- Identification of highly frequent words and subject-specific vocabulary to scaffold students' comprehension of lectures and teaching materials
- The use of L1 in EMI classes
- Identification of language and discourse functions and the way they are used in different modes (written, spoken, electronic) and by different participants (teachers, students) in different languages (English, L1) in EMI
- Awareness of linguistic difficulties of EMI students
- Measuring gains in English proficiency when studying in an EMI programme

Corpus linguistic approaches have been widely used to analyse the language use in various professional and educational contexts (Cheng, 2014; Crawford & Csomay, 2016; Friginal, 2018); therefore, they appear to be well-placed to investigate many of these issues. A corpus is usually defined as a systematically compiled computer-readable collection of naturally occurring written or spoken texts that is sampled to represent a language or language variety which share contextual and situational characteristics (Crawford & Csomay, 2016; Friginal, 2018). Although there are corpora that aim to represent the language use of a whole country or a standard variety, for example, the British National Corpus (BNC) (BNC, 2007) or the Corpus of Contemporary American (COCA; Davies, 2008), the types of corpus that are of interest to EMI are typically specialised corpora that are collections of texts used in various well-defined contexts. Corpora are primarily applied to describe and analyse language forms, functions, and variation by identifying recurring language patterns, for example, frequently co-occurring words as collocations or lexical bundles (Friginal, 2018), and frequently co-occurring linguistic features such as the use of specific syntactic structures or specific pronouns as in multidimensional (MD) analysis (Biber, Conrad, Reppen, Byrd, & Helt, 2002).

Several strengths of corpus approaches to analysing language use have been acknowledged by linguists and applied linguists as the field of corpus linguistics has developed over the last couple of decades (Biber, Conrad, & Reppen, 1998; Friginal, 2018; Crawford & Csomay, 2016). First, researchers recognise the objective power of language corpora as it can provide objective, quantitative data. This kind of objectivity generally makes data analysis more reliable and results verifiable. Reliability is also the result of the use of computers that are less likely to make mistakes in automatic analyses than humans are. The empirical investigation of corpora of authentic, natural texts can produce unambiguous findings – for example, frequency data of particular lexical items – that are not possible by reflection or from subjective accounts of EMI teachers or students. Second, corpus analysis tools can handle a broad range of data. As corpus analyses look for what is typical in the language as a whole, or for a certain register or language variety, it is only feasible if the database that is analysed contains a large amount of data. With corpora of several million running words, these analyses became possible. Third, the many corpus analysis, concordance, and annotating tools that have been developed as computer technology advanced make a broad scope of analysis and an array of different studies possible (Biber et al., 1998).

These strengths of a corpus approach, this chapter will argue, make corpus research appropriate to address many of the language issues identified in EMI and can potentially fill some of the gaps in our knowledge of the language use in EMI. There are, however, surprisingly few corpus studies in EMI; therefore, the present chapter aims to demonstrate the benefits of a corpus approach to the exploration of language use in EMI contexts. To this end the most relevant corpus analytical frameworks and techniques will be discussed. The chapter focuses on three broad areas where corpus research can contribute to EMI research: investigating (1) vocabulary and grammar, (2) spoken classroom and written discourse, and (3) language functions and interaction.

7.2 Focus on vocabulary and grammar

The strengths of corpus approaches to analysing language varieties of the English language are probably most apparent in vocabulary studies. General and specialised corpora have been used to identify the vocabulary that is relevant for learners at specific proficiency levels and for particular disciplines and professions (Nation, 2016). To inform EMI programme developers about the linguistic difficulties students might face, corpus studies that focused on disciplinary vocabulary load and lexical complexity are of specific relevance (Bi, 2020; Briggs, 2017). One very productive research strand in corpus-based vocabulary studies has been the creation of wordlists for general English and English for Specific Purposes (ESP) pedagogic purposes (Nation, 2016). The basic assumption behind such wordlists is that the frequency of vocabulary items is a fairly reliable indicator of usefulness for language learning (Garnier & Schmitt, 2015, p. 647) which is also supported by current theories of language acquisition (Ellis, 2012). The majority of pedagogically motivated vocabulary studies investigated written corpora that typically included textbooks and research articles of the relevant subject fields (Bi, 2020; Yang, 2015). There are a handful of wordlists that were compiled to inform EMI programmes. Bi (2020) – for example, compiled a wordlist for an EMI computer science programme based on the 7.51-million-word Computer Science Textbook Corpus. The wordlist included 356 word families selected according to their range, frequency, and dispersion. The Computer Science Vocabulary List (CSVL) combined with a general wordlist representing students' lexical repertoire acquired from secondary education, provided 95.16% coverage of the corpus. The 95% coverage is often cited as the minimum requirement for reasonable reading comprehension (Laufer, 1989). Other vocabulary lists that have so far been created for EMI contexts analysed spoken corpora (Dang, Coxhead, & Webb, 2017; Rieder-Bünemann, Hüttner, & Smit, 2019). Dang and colleagues (2017) developed the Academic Spoken Word List (ASWL) with the explicit aim to support EMI students' comprehension of academic speech at EMI universities. The wordlist was compiled based on the analysis of a 13-million-word corpus that included recorded and transcribed lectures, seminars, labs, and tutorials of 24 subject fields including hard and soft sciences. The ASWL comprises 1,741 word families that were selected using range, frequency, and dispersion as selection criteria. Wordlists are often criticised for their focus on single-word vocabulary (Jablonkai, 2020). To address this limitation Rieder-Bünemann and colleagues (2019) proposed a holistic model to identify subject-specific vocabulary. The model integrated corpus-linguistic and qualitative data analysis for identifying both single and multi-word lexical units specific to the school subject in oral classroom data.

In addition to preparing subject-specific wordlists corpora can be used to determine the required vocabulary size to read EMI course materials or for adequate comprehension of EMI lectures. Brown and colleagues (2019), for example, tested the New General Service List (NGSL) and the New Academic Word List (NAWL) as study tools for students in an EMI university program. The study used a corpus of approximately 500,000 words of reading texts used in EMI courses. Based on the results, the authors question the appropriateness of the NAWL for their programmes as it only provided an additional 3% coverage beyond that of the NGSL which alone covered 87.7% of the corpus of EMI readings.

Corpora are widely used to analyse the lexical complexity of texts (Johnson, 2017). Lexical complexity is typically analysed in terms of text internal and text external measures. Text internal measures are lexical diversity that gives the ratio of unique words to total number of words and lexical density that measures the ratio of content words to the total number of words (Johnson, 2017). Text external measures such as lexical sophistication is often measured by the percentage of low-frequency words (Lindqvist, Gudmundson, & Bardel, 2013) that are often considered more advanced, difficult, or sophisticated. Wordlists arranged into frequency bands, for example, the BNC/COCA wordlist (Nation, 2017), can be used to determine the coverage of specific words representing specific frequency levels.

To date, there is very little corpus-based research into lexical complexity in EMI, although these are relevant measures to identify the vocabulary load and related linguistic difficulties of EMI students when they read their textbooks or listen to lectures. One of the few exceptions is a study by Briggs (2017) comparing the lexical diversity and the coverage of the Academic Word List (Coxhead, 2000) and general frequency-level wordlists (BNC wordlist, Nation, 2017) in higher education lectures in anglophone and EMI contexts. The study compared vocabulary in the STEM sub-corpora of the British Academic Spoken Corpus (BASE) of 154,856 words of around 20 hours of lectures with the Corpus of Lectures of EMI (CLEMI) of 147,738 words of around 21 hours of lectures by EMI lecturers with Dutch, Spanish, Czech, Italian, and Croatian as their L1s from nine countries (Briggs, 2017). Her results showed that the BASE corpus was significantly more lexically diverse than the CLEMI corpus. The necessary vocabulary sizes to reach 95% and 98% coverage, the levels of reasonable and complete comprehension of reading texts (Hirsh & Nation, 1992), was very high more than 14-thousand-word families of the BNC wordlist (Nation, 2016) in both corpora. If the 90% coverage was considered as the required threshold to adequately comprehend spoken texts as suggested by more recent research (Van Zeeland & Schmitt, 2013) a five-thousand-word-family vocabulary size appeared to be necessary. There seems to be a considerable difference between these estimates; therefore, further studies with a corpus-based approach are needed to identify a more accurate vocabulary size threshold to study in specific EMI programmes.

Another aspect of complexity that corpus studies often focus on is syntactic complexity. Syntactic complexity is usually defined as the degree of sophistication and the variation of the syntactic structures in a text (Lu, 2017). It is typically conceptualised in terms of length of clauses or sentences, clausal complexity that is the amount of subordination and coordination, and the degree of phrasal complexity – for example, the number of prepositional phrases and nouns with postmodifiers (Jin, Lu, & Ni, 2020; Kyle & Crossley, 2018). Syntactic complexity has been widely used to capture L1 and L2 writing development and readability of texts and teaching materials (Lu, 2017; Jin et al., 2020). Different genres and registers were found to demonstrate different levels of complexity and variation in the different measures of complexity. Biber et al. (2002), for example, found that higher phrasal complexity was characteristic of academic writing whereas higher clausal complexity was characteristic of informal conversations. Corpus-based analysis of syntactic complexity of EMI students' written or oral production in different stages of their studies could establish gains in English language development throughout EMI programmes.

7.3 Focus on written and spoken discourse

Corpus methodologies have been used to explore language variation according to social contexts. Register studies, for example, investigate the relationship between language use and context underpinned by a social theory of language positing that language use varies in different social contexts according to the specific communicative goals (Csomay & Wu, 2020, p. 131; Biber, 1988; Biber et al., 2002). Such studies typically follow Biber's (1988) methodology, the multidimensional (MD) analysis, to provide comprehensive linguistic descriptions of registers based on the quantitative analysis of patterns of language variation in corpora. Biber (1988) examined the co-occurrence distribution of 67 linguistic features (e.g., second-person pronouns, causative subordination, *wh*-clauses) across a great number of spoken and written texts with the help of multivariate statistical techniques. He identified five main underlying dimensions which represent the specific linguistic features that co-occur with markedly high frequencies through a statistical factor analysis (e.g., Dimension 1: involved versus informational production, Dimension 2: narrative versus non-narrative discourse).

For the present chapter studies that used MD analysis to registers in educational contexts are of specific relevance. Csomay (2005), for example, applied the MD analytical framework together with text segmentation methods based on the vocabulary used in university classroom discourse in corpora of 196 class sessions of 1.4 million words. She identified three underlying dimensions in higher education classroom discourse: (1) contextual, directive orientation versus conceptual, informational focus, (2) personalised framing versus lack of personalized framing, and (3) interactive dialogue versus teacher monologue. The MD analytical approach in this study shed light upon language variation related to disciplines, levels of instruction, instructional purposes, and class sizes.

In a recent study, Csomay and Wu (2020) compared university classroom language in an anglophone, U.S., and in an EMI, Singapore, context by MD analysis. The U.S. corpus was a subset of the MICASE corpus (Simpson, Lee, & Leicher, 2002) of 103 files, totalling about 730,000 words in three disciplines: humanities, natural science, and engineering. The Singapore corpus comprised 21 files and 193,270 words of recordings of classroom discourse in the same disciplines. Both corpora included a variety of lectures and seminar-style interactive teaching in similar proportions. The texts in both corpora were automatically segmented into vocabulary-based discourse units and were grammatically tagged. The results of the comparison suggested that there are systematic differences between the dimension scores between the two contexts. At the beginning of humanities classes, for example, lecturers in the U.S. context seem to typically use language associated with contextual, directive orientation whereas lecturers in Singapore tend to use language associated with conceptual, informational focus. These differences might be the result of differences in academic culture and pedagogical approaches which bring about differences in information and discourse organisation. EMI studies that apply a corpus-based MD analytical framework can lead to a more nuanced understanding of linguistic features and variation in classroom discourse across different disciplines and educational settings.

A different approach to analyse language use in various contexts is to focus on metadiscourse that is often referred to as the non-propositional functions of language use (Hyland, 2017). In the past few decades researchers have increasingly recognised that language is not exclusively a tool for conveying and exchanging information, but it is employed to organise the information to a specific audience and to facilitate comprehension of the propositions (Hyland, 2017). Corpus methods are often a preferred way to investigate metadiscourse in written and spoken discourse in various contexts. Evidence from such analyses suggested that the metadiscoursal resources that writers and speakers employ are nuanced by the different professional, disciplinary, institutional, and cultural contexts (Lee & Subtirelu, 2015; Lin, 2012; Molino, 2018).

A study by Lee and Subtirelu (2015), for example, compared the metadiscourse in English for Academic Purposes (EAP) classes and subject classes in anglophone contexts represented by the relevant subsets of the second language classroom discourse (L2CD; Lee, 2011) corpus and the MICASE corpus (Simpson et al., 2002). Their findings revealed that metadiscoursal resources are more frequently employed by EAP teachers than subject teachers. EAP teachers use explicit linguistic resources to signal engagement (e.g., inclusive *we*), especially when setting up pedagogical tasks, whereas subject teachers primarily use linguistic expressions that signal transitions and relationships between different stages of the lectures (e.g., coordinating conjunctions: *and*, *but*, and *so*). The use of other metadiscourse features (e.g., hedges, boosters) did not show considerable differences in the two contexts. Similar corpus studies would be needed to extend our understanding of interactional and interactive metadiscourse in EMI contexts. EMI teachers could benefit from a more heightened awareness of the expressions that can be used to help guide students through the content of subject classes and encourage their engagement (Zare & Keivanloo-Shahrestanaki, 2017).

At the same time, EMI students' use of the metadiscoursal resources typical of their profession or discipline can be analysed in their written and spoken production in order to measure the gain in English proficiency especially in terms of their discipline-specific communicative competence. Hafner and Wang (2018), for example, analysed EMI students' use of boosters (e.g., *always*, *obvious*, *clearly*) in their assignments included in the Hong Kong Learner Corpus of Legal Academic Writing in English (HKL-CLAWE). The authors compared students' use of boosters across years of study and findings revealed that the frequency of boosters is lower in final year students' assignments than in assignments of students in earlier years in their studies. Analysis of the use of boosters in professional legal texts revealed that the use of boosters is usually discouraged because of the inherent uncertainty of legal issues in general. Therefore, the findings of the analysis of the HKLCLAWE suggested that students seemed to adjust their use of boosters to disciplinary expectations as they gain a better understanding of disciplinary language use throughout their EMI law studies.

7.4 Focus on discourse functions and interaction

A unique feature and strength of corpus studies is the application of automatic search and analysis of specific pre-defined linguistic metrics based on the frequency of specific words, sequences of words, or syntactic structures in corpora (Friginal, 2018). There is, however, a body of corpus research that employs a combination of automatic searches and qualitative analysis of linguistic aspects of texts. These combined methodologies are often used to analyse discourse functions and aspects of interaction in different contexts (Biber et al., 1998; Lin, 2012). In some of these studies, corpus methods are used to select frequent words or word sequences for further analysis. Jawhar (2012), for example, started her analysis of classroom interaction by identifying the most frequent words in her corpus of 16 hours of EMI classes in the Saudi Arabian higher education context. Corpus methods such as frequency lists and keyword analysis (Scott & Tribble, 2006) were used to select the most relevant words for further analysis. She found that many of the most frequent words were backchannelling items (e.g., *uh, aha, yeah, yes*). The qualitative part of the analysis applied a conversation analytic approach to investigate how teachers and students used the short response *yes* in classroom interaction. Her findings demonstrate how EMI students with limited linguistic resources manage classroom interaction and accomplish relevant interactional functions such as taking the floor and asking for clarification. The frequent use of L1 words was also evidenced in her corpus as words translated from Arabic appeared among the keywords.

Automatic searches in corpora can also identify recurring multi-word sequences (Biber & Barbieri, 2007). One such sequence that has been found characteristic of written and spoken discourse is the construct lexical bundle. Lexical bundles were defined:

> as the most frequent recurring lexical sequences . . . which can be regarded as extended collocations: sequences of three or more words that show a statistical tendency to co-occur (e.g., *in the case of the, do you want me to, I said to him*).
>
> (Biber & Conrad, 1999, p. 183)

Qualitative analysis of lexical bundles in their textual contexts in concordance lines found that they serve specific discourse functions. The three main functions lexical bundles serve are expressing stance; organising discourse; and referring to, for example, specific attributes, time, and place. Lexical bundles proved to be a useful construct to characterise language use in different contexts, modes, and disciplines (Biber & Conrad, 1999; Hyland, 2008). Liu and Chen (2020), for example, analysed the discourse functions of four-word lexical bundles in an 8.8-million-word corpus of 1,130 academic lectures from U.S. universities including four disciplines: engineering, humanities and arts, science and math, and social science. The study confirmed that lexical bundles were associated with academic lectures and were different from lexical bundles of other academic spoken registers thus supporting the idea that lexical bundles are typical of the communicative purposes of registers (Biber & Barbieri, 2007). Lexical bundles, however, did not appear to be discipline-specific. Although the frequencies of lexical bundles varied considerably in disciplines, the actual items used in the different disciplines were similar. Corpus-based EMI studies could identify the relevant language and discourse functions and explore how they are used in different EMI contexts.

7.5 Concluding remarks

This overview aimed to give insights into what a corpus approach and specific corpus methodologies can offer to EMI research. Building on the strengths of corpus methods future studies in EMI could focus on the following language-related issues.

7.5.1 Linguistic demand of EMI programmes

To this end subject- and context-specific corpora comprising EMI teaching materials, textbooks, and subject lectures could be built to measure the linguistic complexity students need to cope with. The lexical coverage of existing frequency-based general wordlists (e.g., BNC/COCA, Nation, 2017) can be measured in such corpora in order to set benchmarks for entering specific EMI programmes and to identify the vocabulary size required for appropriate comprehension of the materials. Subject-specific wordlists can be created to inform preparatory and in-sessional EAP and ESP courses about the vocabulary load of specific EMI programmes they support.

7.5.2 Subject-specific linguistic learning outcomes

Analysis of corpora built to represent disciplinary language use that students in specific EMI programmes need to be prepared for can inform EMI stakeholders about the linguistic aspects of discipline-specific communicative competence. Such analyses can focus on vocabulary, discipline-specific collocations, and the use of metadiscoursal resources.

7.5.3 English language development in EMI programmes

In order to gain a better understanding of the extent and nature of English language development in EMI programmes, learner corpora consisting of students' written and spoken production can be analysed (Johnson, 2017). Such analyses could focus on the change in lexical and syntactic complexity, and gains in terms of discipline-specific language competence by investigating the use of lexical bundles and metadiscoursal resources as indicators of discourse organisation.

7.5.4 Discourse organisation and functions in EMI classroom discourse

As discussed earlier, corpus methods, often in combination with qualitative analyses, can be applied to investigate discourse functions and how language is used in different EMI contexts to express such relevant functions. Explicit teaching of discourse functions and discourse markers can enhance EMI students' comprehension of classes (Zare & Keivanloo-Shahrestanaki, 2017). At the same time, EMI teachers' awareness of such discourse markers can provide useful linguistic means to scaffold student learning (Hyland, 2017; Lee & Subtirelu, 2015). To this end, existing corpora, for example, the English as a Lingua Franca in Academic Settings (ELFA) corpus (Mauranen, Hynninen, & Ranta, 2010) could be analysed and further context-specific corpora can be created to capture the language use in higher education and school EMI contexts. In addition to corpora comprising written texts and transcriptions of lectures, more recent advances in technology allow to build multi-modal corpora where texts, audio, and video-recordings can be aligned for analysis (Adolphs & Carter, 2007). This might be especially important as non-verbal features seem to play an important role in certain discourse functions (e.g., explanations) and they were also found to facilitate comprehension (Morton, 2017). The role of L1 in discourse organisation and functions is a further important aspect that the analysis of EMI corpora could shed light on. For this purpose, multilingual corpora can be compiled in which L1 words and expressions are not translated into English. Previous EMI studies also called for a more globally orientated approach that acknowledges the use of English as a lingua franca (Galloway, Kriukow, & Numajiri, 2017). Future EMI corpus studies should take an approach that fully recognises the role of English in their specific contexts when designing and building their corpora.

The present overview would not be complete without discussing the limitations of corpus approaches. One often-cited challenge of corpus studies is that texts are divorced from their contexts. To address this limitation corpus researchers typically provide metadata with their corpora (O'Keefe & McCarthy, 2010). These usually include background information about the writers or speakers and the context. In some cases, additional projects provide extensive details about the context. The Studying in English as a Lingua Franca (SELF) project (Hynninen, 2010), a follow-up project of building the ELFA corpus, for example, aimed to relate the linguistic analysis to the experiences of the language users and thus complement the corpus approach with a more qualitative and ethnographic perspective.

It should be noted that this overview is by no means exhaustive and there are several other corpus-based analytical frameworks that could be used to investigate language issues in EMI – for example, collocational analysis, corpus pragmatic analyses, and corpus annotation (Crawford & Csomay, 2016; O'Keefe & McCarthy, 2010). Overall, given the demonstrated strengths of corpus research in exploring context-specific language varieties, future EMI research should unlock the potential that corpus linguistics can offer in terms of new perspectives, approaches, and methods.

References

Adolphs, S., & Carter, R. (2007). Beyond the word. New challenges in analysing corpora of spoken English. *European Journal of English Studies*, *41*(2), 113–146.

Bi, J. (2020). How large a vocabulary do Chinese computer science undergraduates need to read English-medium specialist textbooks? *English for Specific Purposes*, *58*, 77–89.

Biber, D. (1988). *Variation across speech and writing*. Cambridge University Press. doi:10.1017/CBO9780511621024

Biber, D., & Barbieri, F. (2007). Lexical bundles in university spoken and written registers. *English for Specific Purposes*, *26*(3), 263–286.

Biber, D., & Conrad, S. (1999). Lexical bundles in conversation and academic prose. In H. Hasselgard, & S. Oksefjell (Eds.), *Out of corpora* (pp. 181–190). Amsterdam: Rodopi.

Biber, D., Conrad, S., & Reppen, R. (1998). *Corpus linguistics: Investigating language structure and use*. New York: Cambridge University Press.

Biber, D., Conrad, S., Reppen, R., Byrd, P., & Helt, M. (2002). Speaking and writing in the university: A multidimensional comparison. *TESOL Quarterly*, *36*(1), 9–48.

Briggs, J. (2017, July 5). *Lexical diversity and coverage in tertiary-level STEM: A corpus-based comparison of English-medium lectures in Anglophone and non-Anglophone contexts*. [video podcast] Retrieved from https://podcasts.ox.ac.uk/lexical-diversity-and-coverage-tertiary-level-stem-corpus-based-comparison-english-medium

Brown, H., Bennett, P., & Stoeckel, T. (2019). General and academic wordlists in English- medium instruction programs. In P. Clements, A. Krause, & P. Bennett (Eds.), *Diversity and inclusion*. (pp. 177–182). Tokyo: JALT.

Cheng, W. (2014). Corpus analyses of professional discourse. In V. Bhatia & S. Bremner (Eds.), *The Routledge handbook of language and professional communication* (pp. 13–25). London: Routledge.

Coxhead, A. (2000). A new academic word list. *TESOL Quarterly, 34*(2), 213–238.

Crawford, W. J., & Csomay, E. (2016). *Doing corpus linguistics*. New York: Routledge.

Csomay, E. (2005). Linguistic variation within university classroom talk: A corpus-based perspective. *Linguistics and Education, 15*(3), 243–274.

Csomay, E., & Wu, S. M. (2020). Language variation in university classrooms A corpus- driven geographical perspective. *Register Studies, 2*(1), 131–165.

Dalton-Puffer, D., & Smit, U. (2013). Content and language integrated learning: A research agenda. *Language Teaching, 46*(4), 545–559.

Dang, T. N. Y., Coxhead, A., & Webb, S. (2017). The academic spoken word list. *Language Learning, 67*(4), 959–997. doi:10.1111/lang.12253

Davies, M. (2008). *The corpus of contemporary American English: 520 million words, 1990- present*. Retrieved from http://corpus.byu.edu/coca/

Ellis, N. C. (2012). Frequency-based accounts of second language acquisition. In S. M. Gass & A. Mackey (Eds.), *The Routledge handbook of second language acquisition* (pp. 193–210). Abingdon: Routledge.

Friginal, E. (2018). *Corpus Linguistics for language teachers*. Abingdon: Routledge.

Galloway, N., Kriukow, J., & Numajiri, T. (2017). *Internationalisation, higher education and the growing demand for English: An investigation into the English medium of instruction (EMI) movement in China and Japan*. ELT Research papers 17.2. British Council. Retrieved from www.teachingenglish.org.uk/sites/teacheng/files/H035%20ELTRA%20Interna   tionalisation_HE_and%20the%20growing%20demand%20for%20English%20A4_FI NAL_WEB.pdf

Garnier, M., & Schmitt, N. (2015). The PHaVE list: A pedagogical list of phrasal verbs and their most frequent meaning senses. *Language Teaching Research, 19*(6), 645–666.

Hafner, C. A., & Wang, S. H. (2018). Hong Kong learner corpus of legal academic writing in English: A study of boosters as a marked language form in an English-Medium Instruction context. *TESOL Quarterly, 52*(3), 680–691.

Hirsh, D., & Nation, P. (1992). What vocabulary size is needed to read unsimplified texts for pleasure? *Reading in a Foreign Language, 8*(2), 689–696.

Hyland, K. (2008). As can be seen: Lexical bundles and disciplinary variation. *English for Specific Purposes, 27*(1), 4–21.

Hyland, K. (2017). Metadiscourse: What is it and where is it going? *Journal of Pragmatics, 113*, 16–29.

Hynninen, N. (2010). "We try to to to speak all the time in easy sentences" – Student conceptions of ELF interaction. *Helsinki English Studies, 6*, 29–43.

Jablonkai, R. R. (2020). Leveraging professional wordlists for productive vocabulary knowledge. *ESP Today, 8*(1), 2–24.

Jawhar, S. (2012). *Conceptualising CLIL in a Saudi context: A corpus linguistic and conversation analytic perspective* (Doctoral dissertation). University of Newcastle Upon Tyne, UK. Retrieved from https://theses.ncl.ac.uk/dspace/bitstream/10443/1849/1/Jawhar12.pdf.

Jin, T., Lu, X., & Ni, J. (2020). Syntactic complexity in adapted teaching materials: Differences among grade levels and implications for benchmarking. *Modern Language Journal, 104*(1), 192–208. doi:10.1111/modl.12622

Johnson, M. D. (2017). Cognitive task complexity and L2 written syntactic complexity, accuracy, lexical complexity, and fluency: A research synthesis and meta-analysis. *Journal of Second Language Writing, 37*, 13–38.

Kyle, K., & Crossley, S. A. (2018). Measuring syntactic complexity in L2 writing using fine-grained clausal and phrasal indices. *Modern Language Journal, 102*(2), 333–349. doi:10.1111/modl.12468

Laufer, B. (1989). What percentage of text lexis is essential for comprehension? In C. Lauren & M. Nordman (Eds.), *Special language: From human thinking to thinking machines* (pp. 316–323). Clevedon: Multilingual Matters.

Lee, J. J. (2011). *A genre analysis of second language classroom discourse: Exploring the rhetorical, linguistic, and contextual dimensions of language lessons* (Unpublished doctoral dissertation). Georgia State University, Atlanta, GA.

Lee, J. J., & Subtirelu, N. (2015). Metadiscourse in the classroom: A comparative analysis of EAP lessons and university lectures. *English for Specific Purposes, 31*, 52–62.

Lin, C. (2012). Modifiers in BASE and MICASE: A matter of academic cultures or lecturing styles? *English for Specific Purposes, 31*(2), 117–126.

Lindqvist, C., Gudmundson, A., & Bardel, C. (2013). A new approach to measuring lexical sophistication in L2 oral production. In C. Bardel, C. Laufer, & C. Lindqvist (Eds.), *L2 vocabulary acquisition, knowledge and use. New perspectives on assessment and corpus analysis* (pp. 109–125). EuroSLA Monographs Series 2. Eurosla, Amsterdam: European Second Language Association.

Liu, C., & Chen, H-J. H. (2020). Analyzing the functions of lexical bundles in undergraduate academic lectures for pedagogical use. *English for Specific Purposes, 58*, 122–137.

Lu, X. (2010). Automatic analysis of syntactic complexity in second language writing. *International Journal of Corpus Linguistics, 15*(4), 474–496. doi:10.1075/ijcl.15.4.02lu

Lu, X. (2017). Automated measurement of syntactic complexity in corpus-based L2 writing research and implications for writing assessment. *Language Testing, 34*(4), 493–511. doi:10.1177/0265532217710675

Macaro, E. (2019). Exploring the role of language in English medium instruction. *International Journal of Bilingual Education and Bilingualism, 23*(3), 263–267.

Macaro, E., Curle, S., Pun, J., An, J., & Dearden, J. (2018). A systematic review of English medium instruction in higher education. *Language Teaching, 51*(1), 36–76.

Mauranen, A., Hynninen, N., & Ranta, E. (2010). English as an academic lingua franca: The ELFA project. *English for Specific Purposes, 29*(3), 183–190.

Molino, A. (2018). 'What I'm Speaking is almost English. . .': A corpus-based study of metadiscourse in English-medium lectures at an Italian university. *Educational Sciences: Theory & Practice, 18*(4), 935–956.

Morton, T. (2017). Vocabulary explanations in CLIL classrooms: A conversation analysis perspective. *The Language Learning Journal, 43*(3), 256–270. doi:10.1 080/09571736.2015.1053283

Nation, I. S. P. (2016). *Making and using word lists for language learning and testing*. Amsterdam: John Benjamins.

Nation, I. S. P. (2017). *The BNC/COCA level 6 word family lists* (Version 1.0.0) [Data file]. Retrieved from www.victoria.ac.nz/lals/staff/paul-nation.aspx

O'Keefe, A., & McCarthy, M. (Eds.). (2010). *The Routledge handbook of corpus linguistics*. London: Routledge.

Rieder-Bünemann, A., Hüttner, J., & Smit, U. (2019). Capturing technical terms in spoken CLIL: A holistic model for identifying subject- specific vocabulary. *Journal of Immersion and Content-Based Language Education, 7*(1), 4–29.

Scott, M., & Tribble, C. (2006). *Textual patterns*. Amsterdam: John Benjamins.

Simpson, R., Lee, D. Y. W., & Leicher, S. (2002). *MICASE manual*. Ann Arbor, MI: University of Michigan Press.

The British National Corpus, version 3 (BNC XML Edition). (2007). Distributed by Bodleian Libraries, University of Oxford, on behalf of the BNC Consortium. Retrieved from www.natcorp.ox.ac.uk/

Van Zeeland, H., & Schmitt, N. (2013). Lexical coverage in L1 and L2 listening comprehension: The same or different from reading comprehension? *Applied Linguistics, 34*(4), 457–479. doi:10.1093/applin/ams074

Yang, M. (2015). A nursing academic word list. *English for Specific Purposes, 37*, 27–38.

Zare, J., & Keivanloo-Shahrestanaki, J. (2017). Genre awareness and academic lecture comprehension: The impact of teaching importance markers. *Journal of English for Academic Purposes, 27*, 31–41.

8 Developing a Collaborative Lesson Planning Tool in EMI

Mustafa Akincioglu and Yuwei Lin

Abstract

Turkey provides EMI researchers with a unique context that has roots of teaching academic subjects formally through languages other than Turkish (L1), going as far back as the mid-19th century. To date, however, lecturers and students still face challenges when teaching/learning through a language other than their L1. This chapter describes a project conducted in Turkey to promote collaboration between content subject teachers and language teachers in EMI classrooms. Language teachers from the English language preparatory programmes and content-subject teachers from disciplinary departments were provided with a Collaborative Lesson Planning Tool in facilitating collaboration between content and language teaching in EMI classrooms. Reflective interviews were conducted to evaluate the usefulness of the collaboration tool. The teachers discussed factors that affected the effectiveness of joint collaboration between content and language teaching and their challenges in teaching at Preparatory Year Programme.

8.1 Introduction

EMI is defined by Macaro (2018) as "the use of the English language to teach academic subjects (other than English itself) in countries or jurisdictions where the first language (L1) of the majority of the population is not English" and has a rapid use rate around the word. Turkey, a country which is positioned in both Europe and Asia, also adopted this teaching method in some higher education institutions. While, nowadays, Turkish lecturers and students still face challenges when teaching/learning through English rather than their first language (L1). In particular, students may complain about their limited English proficiency, causing them to meet the linguistic demand in the classroom and thus create obstacles in their learning process such as understanding of content knowledge

DOI: 10.4324/9781003025115-8

(Macaro, 2018). It provides an opportunity for researchers to re-examine the role of teachers in delivering both content and language teaching at the stage of Preparatory Year Programme (PYP) and how content-subject and language teachers can strategically collaborate at the classroom level in order to eliminate any possible challenges that may arise from EMI teaching.

This chapter describes a project conducted in Turkey to promote collaboration between content subject teachers and language teachers in EMI classrooms. Language teachers from the English language preparatory programmes and content-subject teachers from disciplinary departments were provided with a "Collaborative Lesson Planning Tool" in facilitating collaboration between content and language teaching in EMI classrooms. Reflective interviews were conducted to evaluate the usefulness of the collaboration tool. The teachers discussed factors that affected the effectiveness of joint collaboration between content and language teaching and their challenges in teaching at PYP.

8.2 EMI in Turkey

Teaching content-subject through English is a now growing phenomenon around the world. A significant amount of research evidence has shown that students, parents, and educational institutions welcome the idea of more EMI adoption, and implement EMI in response to the phenomenon that English is a lingua franca which provides prosperity for students and leads to academic success (Dearden, 2015). Besides, English is recognised as a gateway to global mobilisation at higher education (Graddol, 2006), a seal for relatively higher quality education and an access to obtain better domestic or international job opportunities (O'Dowd, 2015). It is not surprising to note that there is a push for the adoption of more EMI instruction in Turkey. EMI was first introduced in Turkey in the early 1950s, based on a policy adopted by the Turkish government that English was recognised as the second language (L2) in Turkey and replaced French as the traditional instructional language. Meanwhile, five interactional schools named "Maarif Schools" were also established in responding to a wider adoption of EMI instruction (Macaro, 2018).

Due to the establishment of "Maarif Schools", the concept of the preparatory year first appeared in these schools in Turkey in 1955. The first year was a preparatory year to help students improve their basic English capacity in order to match the English level required by their further studies in English-only instruction (Macaro, 2018). This preparatory year was abolished in 2004 and replaced by the PYP as the English bridging course in universities for those undergraduates who wish to study through EMI and bridged the gap between secondary education and EMI (Macaro, 2018). It was conducted in Turkey to help students with low levels of English proficiency strive and adapt in an EMI environment (Macaro, 2018).

8.3 Collaboration between language specialists and content specialists

Research into the teacher collaboration between language specialist (i.e., ESL teacher, etc.) and academic subject teacher (i.e., maths teacher, etc.) is abundant particularly in the field of K–12 and most of them mainly focused on the context of CLIL. In the English-speaking world, such as the U.S., in order to explore a more comprehensive approach of cross-curricular teacher collaboration, Wei, Darling-Hammond, Andree, Richardson, and Orphanos (2009) and Marrongelle, Sztajn, and Smith (2013) illustrated that actually these collaboration practices in the U.S. provided some effective methods for both content-subject and language teachers to develop their teaching skills to address their instructional needs. In addition, researchers such as Pawan and Ortloff (2011) and Giles and Yazan (2019) explored the perceptions of language specialists in the context of English for Second Language (ESL) and observed some good examples about how language teachers and content teachers worked collaboratively in US K–12 classrooms. Additionally, Honigsfeld and Dove (2019) provided a comprehensive argument around language specialist and content teacher collaboration. Although within K–12 context, it placed emphasis on Second Language Teacher Education. Another recent work by Senn, McMurtrie, and Coleman (2019) placed a greater attention on developing an effective interdisciplinary lesson planning through the collaborative efforts between a language specialist and a content teacher. In Europe, Pavon, Avila, Gallego, and Espejo (2015) also conducted similar research involving the practice of the collaborative lesson design by language specialists and content teachers in the context of primary CLIL classrooms.

Meanwhile, in the East, abundant research evidence has demonstrated efforts on exploring the benefits of co-planning and the co-teaching mechanism between language specialists (ESL teachers) and content teachers (i.e., science teacher, etc.). Davison (2006) explored the context of elementary school in Hong Kong. In addition, to analyse the relationships between language specialists and content teachers' collaboration and teachers' beliefs and attitudes, Lo (2014) also carried out a 20-month project to compare the beliefs and attitudes of English teachers with subject teachers concerning their roles in content-based instruction (CBI) and cross-curricular collaboration in Hong Kong secondary schools. Research referring to the collaboration between PYP teachers and EMI teachers at tertiary level is still lacking. In the Summer Programme in Oxford in 2014, though the intention of this programme was to help students overcome the challenges brought by the transition between PYP and EMI, participants also raised this point. It is important to note that, at that time, there was limited research on exploring the cooperation between PYP teachers and EMI teachers.

8.4 Teacher collaboration in higher education context

Although there are numerous studies (Byun et al., 2011) on CLIL in Europe, indicating the efficacy levels attained if both content and language teacher collaboration is in place, similar analysis on EMI on such teacher collaboration is lacking, particularly for tertiary education. Moreover, while CLIL was widely observed to be clearly articulated in the educational policies (Aguilar & Munoz, 2013; Lasagabaster, 2011) and university policymakers' attention was attracted by EMI (Byun et al., 2011). Additionally, students' preparedness level for their academic study has been widely ignored to a great extent. This crucial point was pointed out by the Summer Programme 2014 in Oxford which demonstrated that the departments of PYP and academic subject in EMI universities commonly considered that EMI students had different priorities and "instructional tasks" in terms of language preparedness. That was to say, PYP teachers and managers aimed to ensure that their programmes bring students' levels of English up to CEFR B1 or B2, so that the only task of EMI teachers was effectively delivering the academic content. However, as pointed out in the Summer Programme 2014 in Oxford, the student transition from PYP to EMI programmes has been ignored for a long time by the EMI university stakeholders, causing a negative effect on students learning efficiency.

Due to lacking reliable EMI policies in EMI universities, a number of issues inevitably appeared and needed to be solved. Establishing a completed EMI policy system may provide guidance and protocols for the university stakeholders. Interestingly, a similar view also has been articulated in a recent report on language policies by the League of European Research Universities (LERU, 2019). Briefly, LERU has recently conducted a research project on language policies in some LERU member universities. Based on the findings of this research, LERU reported that the strategic decision of implementing EMI has not found a place in policy documentation. Consequently, without the guidance of policy protocols, it was hard for EMI university stakeholders ensure the quality assurance processes. Furthermore, the LERU report (2019) concerning language policy recommended that effective continued professional development trainings needed to be available for the EMI university stakeholders, so that quality assurance could be designed and implemented successfully.

When it comes to the particular area of cross-curricular and departmental teacher collaboration in the context of EMI universities, it should be taken into consideration that, unlike CLIL K–12 context, EMI universities are not only short on relevant policies but they also lack relevant protocols and guidance that might motivate collaboration and provide assistance for students during their transition from PYP to academic subject learning. That is to say, from a different angle, PYP teachers and EMI teachers were not guided well on students' transitions from PYP to EMI programmes at EMI university policy level in their work contexts. Therefore, within the constraints of their limited authority and resources, both PYP teachers and EMI teachers could make some changes within their power, including initiating some form of cross-departmental collaborations.

In summary, the areas of cross-curricular and departmental collaboration with a focus on EMI students' transitions from PYP to EMI academic subject courses presented a novel challenge not only for researchers but also for policymakers, programme managers, and teachers. Based on the outcomes of the Summer Programme 2014 in Oxford, a new project was designed and conducted. It could be considered as one of the pioneering research projects which has reference value for researchers, EMI university stakeholders, and teachers on students' transitions from PYP to EMI courses, cross-curricular and departmental collaboration between teachers, EMI policy and quality assurance, and so on.

8.5 An intervention: collaboration between a PYP teacher and an EMI teacher

The Summer Programme 2014 in Oxford implemented two research projects, one of which aimed to investigate the collaboration between the PYP teachers and EMI teachers, which placed emphasis on students' transitions from PYP to their academic subject study. In the design process of this research project, a group of researchers at EMI Centre for Research and Development at University of Oxford hypothesised that if there were an effective collaboration between PYP teachers and EMI teachers, a better understanding of the difficulties faced by university students on EMI courses could be gained (Macaro, Dearden, & Akincioglu, 2016).

It is a commonly observed practice that, before the beginning of the new programme years, PYP teachers often communicate with teachers and managers from the academic subject departments. A needs analysis interview is conducted and its results will eventually be used for the PYP course development work. Lesson observations and interviews with students seldom take place during the year and the findings feed into, mostly, the following year's programme development efforts, providing a different angle to this practice of departmental collaboration. In the design of this research project, the goal was to obtain a better understanding of the students' demands during their transition from PYP to EMI courses. In order to achieve this, a collaborative angle was strategised to be opened, which may provide a better insight for the EMI university stakeholders and present practical value in terms of its effective application by both PYP teachers and EMI teachers. Consequently, this collaborative angle was translated into two research questions that ultimately guided this project:

1   How does the collaboration in planning evolve between a PYP teacher and an EMI teacher?
2   What factors make collaboration successful or less successful?

Then a collaborative planning project was designed in order to explore how the collaboration between PYP teachers and EMI teachers in lecture planning evolved and whether teachers would gain mutual benefits from this collaboration. This project was implemented in five EMI universities in Turkey. One of them was the control group, while the other four were the experimental groups. Ten pairs of collaborating PYP teachers and EMI teachers from these schools took part with nine of the pairs completing the collaborative project. EMI teacher peers were selected based on the criteria that they were teaching their academic subjects to first-year EMI students as the majority of whom would come directly from the PYP. Resultantly, the data collected from this study had a greater focus on the effectiveness of the PYP and showed the linguistic preparation levels for the academic subjects taught in the first year.

Initially, one of the researchers visited all the participants in order to explain what was expected from them, provide clarification on the purpose and use of the research tools, and answer any further questions. These collaborating pairs were expected to plan eight subsequent lessons in half a semester. Additionally, the expected sequence and requirements of the collaborative planning session were as follows (Macaro et al., 2016).[1]

1   Each collaborating pair reaches an agreement on their working calendar
2   EMI teachers send the materials which will be used in the lecture to their cooperative PYP teachers
3   PYP teachers list some key linguistic challenges concerning lexical and during the collaborative planning sessions, PYP and EMI teachers discuss how to overcome these linguistic challenges
4   EMI teachers modify the language content of the lecture
5   EMI teachers deliver the planned lectures
6   In the subsequent planning session, EMI teachers provide feedback about the delivered lecture to their cooperative PYP teachers

One of our researchers carried out a total of 18 pre- and post-audio-recorded interviews with the collaborating pairs. Also, all of the collaborating pairs were expected to audio-record each session while keeping a record of their written communication (i.e., email exchanges, handwritten notes, and so on). Compared with the K–12 CLIL context, the university contexts have considerable differences and more challenges on cross-curricular and departmental teacher collaboration because universities present a wider range of academic programmes in all the education they offered. Furthermore, K–12 CLIL context has relatively straightforward educational objectives in which cross-curricular collaboration could play a more natural role. These working principles of effective collaboration in K–12 CLIL context have a reference value for devising an effective collaborative model for the university context. As Davison (2006) suggested, clear conceptualisation of collaborative tasks – and the establishment of monitoring, evaluation, and feedback – were working principles of the collaboration model in the K–12 CLIL context. Moreover, Lo (2014) also demonstrated that opting for a higher level of collaborative model, which required establishing clear roles and responsibilities towards a shared educational objective, could bring the dynamism which was needed for a sustainable and effective collaboration between PYP teachers and EMI teachers over a period of time.

Based on this analysis, a Collaborative Planning Tool (CPT) was designed in order to provide a framework to gain a mutual agreement on task projects, task objectives, processes of monitoring, evaluation and feedbacks, as well as a set road map of collaboration to collaborating peers.

8.6 Collaborative Planning Tool (CPT): a framework for EMI teacher collaboration

As the research tool, the CPT, with a main focus on the lexical content of the lectures, includes prompts and questions to help the collaborating pairs reflect on the language content of the lecture (see online appendix of the published paper). Supported by the research data, the efficacy of CPT provided enough prompts for these collaborative pairs so that they developed a routine quickly for the three key collaboration stages – namely how they are prepared for the collaborative planning session; how they interact during the collaborative planning session; and how they share comments, evaluation, and feedback in the following collaborative planning sessions. This routine was developed by the participants in the project which showed the importance of the collaborative pairs because this routine was a result of agreed objectives of the tasks and the collaboration between these pairs provided a platform for all the participants to negotiate.

In addition, CPT had successfully attained its original target to provide a research framework for all the research project participants. As the research interview data showed, pairs who followed the framework during their collaborative planning sessions felt they gain more understanding of CPT until the third session, and after it they felt they had gradually gained and internalised a better understanding of this framework. Therefore, although they had the printed version at the table in front of them, they did not need to closely follow the prompts from CPT. Interestingly, most of the EMI teachers who participated in this collaborative planning study reported that during the period of delivering the lessons, they had planned collaboratively with their PYP teacher peers within framework/CPT in their minds visually and/or its sequence of the prompts. Another interesting point reported by some EMI teachers was that they realised during the trial they had started to think more systematically about the linguistic needs of their students in the pre-lessons, and post-lessons they delivered with CPT. It can be argued that CPT played a significant role to a great extent while EMI teachers collaborated with their PYP peers concerning the collaborative lesson planning.

As mentioned earlier, the pre- and post-intervention interviews with the EMI teachers who planned lessons collaboratively with their PYP peers by making use of CPT were conducted. Data from the post-intervention interviews that had a particular focus on the use and efficacy of CPT, which showed the following (Macaro et al., 2016):

1   The use and benefits of the CPT
2   The collaboration with PYP teachers in terms of

    a   effective planning with better awareness of language issues
    b   understanding the work finished in PYP better
    c   gaining a self-awareness of their language competence

3   The continuation of collaborative planning with PYP teachers in the future

In terms of the results of the research involving PYP teachers and EMI teachers, these categories are indeed significant. In other words, an effective and well-strategised framework assisted both PYP teachers and EMI teachers in terms of developing a greater focus on their students' linguistic needs. This is important because, as discussed in the earlier paragraphs, PYP teachers and EMI teachers do not generally tend to share a sustained collaborative task to gain a better understanding of students' linguistic demands during their transition from PYP to academic subject study. Therefore, CPT, as an effective framework, successfully provided a platform on which collaborating pairs could develop a shared/negotiated understanding of task objectives, required processes, and roles and responsibilities. Hence, not surprisingly, a number of the EMI teachers also reported that because of this study, they had learnt a lot from their PYP peers. It is extremely important that the EMI teachers' view referring to PYP teachers could also be positively changed by an effective use of a collaborative framework like CPT.

Another important outcome of this collaborative planning study is that EMI teachers who participated in it commonly reported that they saw benefits from continuing "collaboration" with PYP teachers in the future. This is important because the future collaboration is expected to continue, on account that the collaborative experience has yielded positive outcomes for paired participants. Normally, the concept of cross-departmental and curricular collaboration is popular in the university context. Nevertheless, a sustained experience of collaboration between academic subject departments and PYP has been somewhat lacking.

8.7 Limitations

Although this collaborative planning study achieved lots of successful outcomes, it still had some certain limitations. First, only pre- and post-interviews with the EMI teachers were conducted because of constraints of the project resources. Certainly, conducting pre- and post-study interviews with both PYP teachers and EMI teachers would be more informative particularly on the use of CPT. Second, the audio-recordings within their transcripts and the documented written communication between the pairs were also collected. A detailed analysis of this data was needed because it could provide a deeper insight into how PYP teachers' understanding and thinking evolved throughout the study.

Furthermore, although some EMI teachers were willing to record their collaborative planned lessons for data analysis, it was hard to gain the consent from all the EMI teachers. Hence, in order to keep a certain number of the collaborating pairs, the video-recording was not required. However, undoubtedly, video-recording of lessons could provide better insight into the lesson delivery if the team-teaching or observations were not planned for in a study based on the collaborative work. Ultimately, due to the constraints of the available resources and the lack of volunteer participants, an academic-discipline-based category was missing in this study, which could enable researchers to analyse the research data including whether academic discipline based on the emergence of linguistic issues. For the structure and efficacy of CPT, this data was also important.

8.8 Conclusion

A study was carried out in the Turkish Higher Education context in order to find out whether a cross-curricular and departmental collaboration between PYP teachers and EMI teachers who had varying backgrounds might bring about changes in content delivery to create a more assistive nature for the EMI students who are in their transition from PYP to academic subject study. The core objective of this study was understanding the potential of positive impacts well on teaching and learning of the designed collaboration model for this particular purpose. This point was also highlighted by Macaro et al. (2016, p. 69):

> It is clear from the data collected pre- and post-intervention that the project had varying levels of success. . . . Interestingly, it seems that it was those pairs that used the CPT (even if only to some extent) for the purpose for which it was intended who had the most positive experiences and moved forward with their thinking.

According to the research data, it can be argued strongly that a cross-curricular and departmental collaboration model designed particularly for the higher education EMI context could yield positive outputs in terms of quality content delivery. In this model, this study also demonstrated that a framework like CPT could provide invaluable assistance with collaborating peers.

Based on the research data, a more inclusive approach of cross-curricular and departmental collaboration may have a wider-scale positive impact on teaching and learning in the context of EMI universities. That was to say, managers of PYP as well as EMI academic subject departments could also be involved in this process of collaboration for a more effectively sustained development of quality content delivery. This cross-curricular and departmental collaboration approach, particularly focusing on helping EMI students in their transitions from PYP to academic subject study, could be more effective if its principles were translated into an internal Continued Professional Development (CPD) programme.

It is worthwhile to mention that this innovative study was carried out in the higher education context of Turkey and also built the first step for a series of EMI universities symposia in Turkey under the title of "EMI Universities Symposia: A Holistic Approach". These symposia brought multiple stakeholders together, namely policymakers, managers, teachers, students, and alumni and business world representatives of EMI universities in Turkey with the purpose of providing a platform for a holistic approach to EMI universities.

Interestingly, when the proposal was made for some policymakers at Turkish universities in order to organise these symposia in Turkey, the key outcomes of the collaboration study and findings about the efficacy of CPT inspired all the researchers. Resultantly, an equalitarian platform was offered for discussions, including a cross-departmental approach to the ongoing issues of EMI at universities, to all the stakeholders (varying from vice-chancellor to PYP teacher). Providing clear objectives, sharing the ownership of the discussions, and providing equal say in the workshops where the EMI stakeholders were homogeneously presented enabled us to complete four symposia successfully between 2018 and 2019 with more than 100 EMI universities and more than 800 EMI university stakeholders.

According to the research data and the success of the four "EMI Universities Symposia: A Holistic Approach" completed in Turkey, the Collaborative Planning Tool (CPT) has proved to be successful not only in terms of providing a framework for the collaborative peers but also in giving initial and positive examples regarding how cross-departmental collaboration may be initiated and sustained in the EMI university context. Ultimately, the first version of the CPT devised and used in this project has great potential to be developed in the future. Therefore, further research and development on this particular framework/CPT was welcomed and invited.

Note

1 Please refer to Macaro et al. (2016) for detailed information on the collaborative planning research project.

References

Aguilar, M., & Munoz, C. (2013). The effect of proficiency on CLIL benefits in Engineering students in Spain. *International Journal of Applied Linguistics, 24*(1), 1–18.

Byun, K., Chu, H., Kim, M., Park, I., Kim, S., & Jung, J. (2011). English-medium teaching in Korean higher education: Policy debates and reality. *Higher Education, 62*(4), 431–449.

Davison, C. (2006). Collaboration between ESL and content teachers: How do we know when we are doing it right? *International Journal of Bilingual Education and Bilingualism, 9*(4), 454–475.

Dearden, J. (2015). *English as a medium of instruction – A growing global phenomenon.* Retrieved from https://www.britishcouncil.org/sites/default/files/e484_emi_-_cover_option_3_final_web.pdf.

Giles, A., & Yazan, B. (2019). ESL and content teachers' collaboration. *Indonesian Journal of English Language Teaching, 14*(1), 1–18.

Graddol, D. (2006). *English next.* London: British Council.

Honigsfeld, A., & Dove, M. G. (2019). Preparing teachers for co-teaching and collaboration. In L. C. de Olivera (Ed.), *The handbook of TESOL in K-12* (pp. 405–422). Oxford: Wiley-Blackwell.

Lasagabaster, D. (2011). English achievement and student motivation in CLIL and EFL settings. *Innovation in Language Learning and Teaching, 5*(1), 3–18.

League of European Research University (LERU), Language Policies at the LERU member institutions. 2019 [report on the Internet]. Belgium; LERU; 2019 November [about 48 screens].

Lo, Y. Y.(2014). Collaboration between L2 and content subject teachers in CBI: Contrasting beliefs and attitudes. *RELC Journal, 45*, 181–196.

Macaro, E. (2018). *English medium instruction.* Oxford: Oxford University Press.

Macaro, E., Dearden, J., & Akincioglu, M. (2016). English-medium instruction in universities: A collaborative experiment in Turkey. *Studies in English Language Teaching, 4*(1), 51–76.

Marrongelle, K., Sztajn, P., & Smith, M. (2013). Scaling up professional development in an era of common state standards. *Journal of Teacher Education, 64*(3), 202–211.

O'Dowd, R. (2015). *The training and accreditation of teachers for English Medium Instruction: A survey of European universities.* Retrieved July 2015, from http://sgroup.be/sites/default/files/EMI%20Survey_Report_ODowd.pdf

Pavon, V. V., Avila, L. J., Gallego, S. A., & Espejo, M. R. (2015). Strategic and organizational considerations in planning content and language integrated learning: A study on the coordination between content and language teachers. *International Journal of Bilingual Education and Bilingualism, 18*(4), 409–425.

Pawan, F., & Ortloff, J. H. (2011). Sustaining collaboration: English-as-a-second-language, and content-area teachers. *Teaching and Teacher Education, 27*(2), 463–471.

Senn, G., McMurtrie, D., & Coleman, B. (2019). Collaboration in the middle: Teachers in interdisciplinary planning. *Current Issues in Middle Level Education, 24*(1), 24–27.

Wei, R. C., Darling-Hammond, L., Andree, A., Richardson, N., & Orphanos, S. (2009). *Professional learning in the learning profession: A status report on teacher development in the U.S. and abroad.* Dallas, TX: National Staff Development Council.

9 Researching translanguaging in EMI classrooms

Kevin W.H. Tai

Abstract

There is a growing interest in the field of translanguaging in EMI classrooms and the majority of the studies tend to employ functional discourse analysis and ethnographic observations to understand the nature of translanguaging practices in EMI classrooms. However, there is a lack of studies which explicate the detailed processes of how translanguaging practices are realised in EMI classrooms for promoting content and language learning. This chapter explores the possibility of combining Multimodal Conversation Analysis (MCA) and an ethnographic approach in order to better understand how translanguaging practices are realised in EMI classrooms and how translanguaging can facilitate content and language learning in an EMI context. Preliminary analysis from my feasibility trial, which is carried out in Hong Kong EMI secondary mathematics lessons, will be employed to illustrate the arguments. This chapter will argue that MCA can be used to discover the complex multilingual and multimodal resources employed by the interactants in co-constructing meanings through translanguaging in EMI classroom interactions. Moreover, using an ethnographic approach to complement the MCA analysis can potentially allow translanguaging researchers to understand how the wider sociocultural contexts and the identities of the participants play a role in affecting the participants' own translanguaging practices.

9.1 Introduction

Current translanguaging research in EMI and CLIL classrooms tends to employ functional discourse analysis (e.g., Duarte, 2019; Lin & Lo, 2017) and ethnography (e.g., Mazak & Herbas-Donoso, 2015; Lin & He, 2017) to explore how teachers and bilingual learners communicate and create meaning through translanguaging. Very few studies (e.g., Moore, 2014; Lin &

DOI: 10.4324/9781003025115-9

Wu, 2015) have employed conversation analysis to conduct a detailed, line-by-line, fine-grained analysis of the classroom talk in order to analyse the functions that translanguaging serves in EMI and CLIL classrooms. This chapter explores the possibility of combining MCA and an ethnographic approach in order to better understand how translanguaging practices are realised in EMI classrooms and how translanguaging can facilitate knowledge construction in an EMI context. I will draw on the preliminary analysis from my PhD feasibility trial, which is carried out in a Hong Kong (HK) EMI secondary mathematics classroom, to illustrate my arguments. This chapter will argue that MCA can be used to allow researchers to discover the complex multilingual and multimodal resources employed by the interactants in co-constructing meanings through translanguaging in EMI classroom interactions. Moreover, using an ethnographic approach can potentially allow researchers to understand how the wider sociocultural contexts and the identities of the participants play a role in affecting the participants' own translanguaging practices.

9.2 The study

My PhD research, funded by the Economic and Social Research Council, aims to conduct a linguistic ethnographic investigation in HK EMI secondary mathematics and history classrooms. Methodologically, this study integrates MCA with an ethnographic approach. MCA is different from conventional MCA since MCA focuses on the multimodal dimension of talk-in-interaction (e.g., the use of gestures; Mondada, 2019). This unique combination involves observing participant's pedagogical practices over time, as well as understanding the teachers' reflections on classroom practices. This study will explore how translanguaging is employed to achieve the teachers' pedagogical goals at particular moments in the lessons and how teachers' understandings of their translanguaging practices are articulated through interviews. The findings can potentially offer an empirical basis for developing translanguaging as an alternative approach to current EMI policy and practice and discovering the classroom conditions required for the translanguaging practices to succeed. This allows teachers to employ translanguaging to achieve their pedagogical goals, bridge communication gaps and empower the learners.

As part of my doctoral research, I conduct a feasibility trial which entails a two-week linguistic ethnographic investigation in HK secondary EMI mathematics classrooms. This study aims to explore: (1) how translanguaging is employed to achieve pedagogical goals at a particular moment in the EMI lesson and (2) how the mathematics teacher makes sense of his translanguaging practices. The findings of the study are disseminated into a number of research papers (e.g., Tai & Li, 2020a, 2020b, 2020c).

9.2.1 Research planning and design

When I was designing my PhD study, there are several fundamental issues that I considered. In the following sub-sections, I describe the three issues and my responses to them.

The definition of translanguaging

The term "translanguaging" originally used to describe a pedagogical practice of moving flexibly between different input and output languages in Welsh revitalisation classrooms (Williams, 1994). In this situation, the changing of the language is strategic and deliberate instead of spontaneous. The initial aims of translanguaging are to employ the stronger language to help learners to develop the weaker language in order to contribute to the balanced development of the learner's two languages. However, recent translanguaging literature has paid attention to teachers' deployment of multiple linguistic resources for scaffolding. The findings of the studies (e.g., Hornberger & Link, 2012; Li, 2014; Lin & He, 2017) typically indicate that the teachers encourage students to draw on their multilingual and multimodal resources in the classroom which consequently can facilitate the students' development of multilingualism.

One of the most frequently asked questions in the field of applied linguistics is how translanguaging analysis differs from codeswitching analysis. As one argues, the notion of translanguaging emphasises that it not only implies a move between different linguistic structures, systems, and modalities, but also goes beyond linguistic codes and is therefore distinct from the phenomenon of codeswitching. Thus translanguaging is a process of meaning-making which entails the speakers strategically as well as spontaneously drawing on their one linguistic and semiotic repertoire in an integrated manner without focusing on "languages" as distinct and separate codes.

Translanguaging as a theoretical framework has recently encouraged EMI and CLIL researchers to analyse the tension between English as the only language in the classrooms and the reality of multilingual students speaking multiple languages in the classrooms to facilitate the meaning-making processes (Macaro, 2018). Unfortunately, many researchers have not fully understood the ramifications of the notion and there is a tendency for recent research to treat translanguaging as "a re-branding of code-switching"

(Nikula & Moore, 2019, p. 3). For example, Coyle, Hood, and Marsh (2010, p. 16) introduce "blended instruction" in CLIL lessons through translanguaging which is defined as "a systematic shift from one language to another". Although this definition of translanguaging aligns with the original Welsh model of translanguaging which perceives the switching between languages as systematic, a more contemporary take on translanguaging practices will consider them as not only strategic and systematic but also "spontaneous, impromptu and momentary" (Li, 2011, p. 1224). Macaro (2018, p. 215) notes that the notion of translanguaging, in related to EMI or foreign language contexts, "centres on whether bilinguals have separate linguistic codes or a single code in which the languages are meshed together and from which they select strategically in order to communicate". Macaro further argues that his reading of translanguaging literature is that "there are no guidelines on the functions and distribution of the first language (L1) and second language (L2) in the classroom" (p. 215). Such perspective only focuses on the notion of translanguaging as the simple switching between named languages. Moreover, several EMI and CLIL studies, such as Gierlinger's (2015) and Lo's (2015) studies on teachers' use of L1 in EMI and CLIL classrooms, acknowledge translanguaging but the authors frame their discussions of the findings around codeswitching. Hence, this shows that the notion of translanguaging might be mentioned in passing in the EMI and CLIL literature, but the studies mentioned previously do not deploy translanguaging as an analytical perspective (Li, 2018) to inform their data analysis.

As there are various interpretations of the meaning of translanguaging in the field of applied linguistics, researchers can often feel uncertain of how to respond to the theoretical shifts when designing their studies. I argue that it is important for researchers to understand how the notion of translanguaging has developed over time. A clear working definition of translanguaging is also needed in the study in order to allow the researcher to determine what interactional features can be identified as translanguaging. For my PhD project, I adopt a more contemporary take on translanguaging and follow Li's (2011) proposal in order to better capture the complexity of translanguaging practices. I therefore view translanguaging as a process of knowledge construction which involves going beyond different linguistic structures and systems (i.e., not only different languages and dialects but also styles, registers, and other variations in language use) and different modalities (e.g., switching between speaking and writing, or coordinating gestures, body movements, facial expressions, visual images). This definition goes beyond the traditional view of translanguaging which only focuses on the individuals' deployment of multiple linguistic resources for meaning-making (e.g., Garcia, 2009). This will allow me to examine how EMI teachers make use of their multilingual and multimodal repertoires both strategically and spontaneously to achieve the pedagogical goals of the classroom interaction, and how the teachers interact between different modalities and transcend the boundaries of language in the teaching process. I also take the position that speakers draw on their multilingual and multimodal repertoires, as well as other sociocultural dimensions, including the speakers' social identities, life histories, beliefs, and their knowledge of the wider sociocultural environment, as resources in the process of negotiation of meaning.

9.2.2 Methodological framework: combining multimodal conversation analysis with an ethnographic approach

Linguistic ethnography (LE) is one of the most favourable research frameworks for studying the nature of translanguaging in everyday settings (e.g., Creese & Blackledge, 2010) and classroom settings (e.g., Li, 2014). My PhD employs LE as the overall methodological framework. LE is a methodology which "marries" (Wetherell, 2007) linguistics and ethnography to conduct fine-grained studies of social interactions in specific contexts in order to "understand the social processes we are involved in" (Rampton, 2007, p. 12) and how these interactions are embedded in the wider social structures and communicative contexts. It affords the possibility of a linguistic analysis (e.g., discourse analysis) to "tie ethnography down" and "open up" linguistic analysis (Rampton, 2006, p. 395) without excluding ethnographic data so that the strengths of each complement the weaknesses of the other. Through rich description, the employment of audio/video data, a range of ethnographic interview data and other textual documents, the researchers can better understand how language is employed by people in ongoing communicative activity and situated social action and what information this can provide us regarding the wider social constraints, structures, and ideologies (Copland & Creese, 2015).

Multimodal conversation analysis

MCA is employed in my feasibility trial to seek a more fine-grained analysis of interaction than may be achieved with purely ethnographic methods. MCA takes an emic/participant-relevant approach (Markee & Kasper, 2004) in order to explicate the detailed process of how social actions, such as learning, are co-organised and achieved through talk-in-interaction. MCA has developed detailed transcription conventions which enables the analyst to illustrate a high level of granularity of verbal and non-verbal conducts (Jefferson, 2004; Mondada, 2019). MCA allows researchers to analyse naturally occurring interaction and every minute detail is crucial in uncovering participants' orientations towards the interaction.

Collecting ethnographic information

The present study is distinct from a "pure" CA study, which aims to "explicate the endogenous organisation of talk-in-interaction as such" (ten Have, 2001, p. 3), in that it draws on ethnographic data to triangulate with the classroom interaction analysis. The complementarity of MCA with ethnographic approaches has been taken up by researchers elsewhere (e.g., Copland, 2011; Moore & Vallejo, 2018; Matsumoto, 2018). However, the ethnographic information needs to be treated with caution. Several MCA scholars (e.g., Antaki, 2012; Ford, 2012) argued that the goal of MCA is to analyse "what is publicly transacted, not what is privately thought or felt" (Antaki, 2012, p. 497). This is because MCA analyses do not aim to document the speakers' concerns (e.g., worries, intentions, objectives) which are knowable only to the speakers themselves. The primary aim of MCA is to document the observable resources that speakers employ in constructing their actions in interactions. Moreover, the participants' re-interpretations of their actions may range from descriptions of the conversations, the speakers' own interpretations of interactional moments, speakers' own interests, agendas, and concerns and so on. These various types of reports may or may not be relevant in interpreting what happens in the interaction (Pomerantz, 2012) because they may not be publicly displayed in the social interaction. As I was planning to draw on both MCA and ethnographic insights, I became uncomfortable framing my project as a CA study. I was concerned that MCA researchers would challenge my work for not being "CA enough" and that ethnographic researchers would reject my work for being too "micro-analytic".

Despite these arguments regarding the use of ethnographic information (e.g., interview data) to inform MCA analyses, Ford (2012, p. 511) further points out: "for non-CA research agendas in which CA is used as one method", participants' self-reports are sources for understanding their concerns, ideologies, and the potential links between the retrospective recalls and the real-time interactions. For studying research topics like translanguaging practices in EMI classrooms, gathering ethnographic information makes absolute sense to complement the MCA analysis of the classroom interactions. It is particularly important to collect both observation and recording of classroom interactions and teacher's metalanguaging data (i.e., commentaries on the teacher's language practices as lived experience; Li, 2011) in order to understand the construction of translanguaging practices in the EMI classrooms. MCA cannot reveal how participants bring various dimensions of personal history, ideologies, beliefs, and so on, to create the translanguaging spaces in EMI classrooms. These sociocultural factors can only be explored through using an ethnographic approach.

Hence, collecting ethnographic data (e.g., interviews and field notes) potentially allows me to gather contextual information to inform the interpretations of my MCA analysis. (Copland, 2011; Matsumoto, 2018). Seedhouse (2004) argues that although combining MCA and ethnography can allow researchers to link the macro-levels of contextual and social structures with the micro-level of linguistic practices. However, any analytical claim about the interactions needs to be based on the participants' orientations as evidenced in the details of the talk.

Using discourse analysis versus multimodal conversation analysis for analysing EMI classroom interactions

Although there are a number of studies which combine discourse analysis (DA) with an ethnographic approach to explore translanguaging in EMI and CLIL classrooms (e.g., Mazak & Carroll, 2016; Lin & He, 2017; Probyn, 2019) and in other bilingual classrooms (e.g., Creese & Blackledge, 2010; Li, 2014; Wang, 2019), these studies fail to conduct a detailed, line-by-line, fine-grained analysis of classroom talk in order to analyse the functions of translanguaging served in the classrooms. It is crucial to note that DA serves as an umbrella term with a focus "on talk and text as social practice, and on the resources that are drawn on to enable practice" and the logic of DA consists a rhetorical move and a norm (Potter, 1996, p. 31). The rhetorical move is related to categorisation and the norm to accounts or sanctions. The central concept of DA is function. Functions are speech acts, in that functions are concerned with "what that piece of language is doing, or how the listener/reader is supposed to react" (McCarthy, 1991, p. 9). In addition, particular units are related to language forms, including grammatical, lexical, and phonological ones (McCarthy, 1991). In this sense, in DA, there is a form-function mapping. Furthermore, DA favours "coding and category system" (Psathas, 1995, p. 9) which requires researchers to analyse classroom discourse in structural-functional linguistic terms. Nonetheless, the DA approach massively oversimplifies the social interaction since the interaction has to be coded as a single instructional sequence or as a single move in order to fit into the coding scheme (Seedhouse, 2004).

MCA is used in my feasibility trial because it allows researchers to conduct fine-grained analysis to analyse how multilinguals use the different resources available to them (language, artefacts, body movements) to design their actions and recognise these actions (e.g., Matsumoto, 2018; Tai & Brandt, 2018; Tai & Khabbazbashi, 2019a, 2019b). MCA adopts an emic or participant-relevant perspective on social action (Markee & Kasper, 2004). This analytic stance offers the study of learner-learner or expert-novice interactions without pre-theorising the relevance and importance of language-in-use, which includes semiotic resources such as gesture and body posture (Firth & Wagner, 1997). As MCA relies on the participants' perspective (or participants' observable interactional orientations), this analytical approach can allow me to investigate how participants orient to the normativity of language use when they are engaging in translanguaging.

Since I am interested in understanding how translanguaging is employed in particular moments of the EMI mathematics classroom interactions, using MCA mechanism will also allow me to first discover a broad description of different kinds of interactional contexts in the EMI classrooms. In this feasibility trial, pedagogical goals are not referring to descriptions of what the student will be able to do after the lesson. As Walsh (2011, p. 111) argues, pedagogical goals "are manifested in the talk-in-interaction". Classroom talk can be considered as being goal-oriented since classroom participants are striving towards some institutional goals. In this case, the institutional goal in EMI classrooms is to teach the learners the content subjects through English (the L2). In this study, the teacher's pedagogical goals (e.g., eliciting, explaining, setting up activities, giving feedback, carrying out direct instruction) are referring to the teacher's intention to carry out classroom activities in specific moments in the classroom interaction. Therefore, this study draws on the concept of classroom micro-contexts (i.e., sub-varieties of the classroom interaction), which is developed by Seedhouse (2004) to investigate how translanguaging contributes to the creation of different classroom micro-contexts in EMI mathematics lessons.

9.2.3 Methodology in detail

The feasibility trial is conducted at a HK EMI secondary school for two weeks. It involves one EMI mathematics teacher teaching a junior and a senior secondary mathematics class. Classroom interaction data is collected from two mathematics classrooms, which are taught by the same teacher. The data is transcribed using the conventions developed by Jefferson (2004) and Mondada (2019) to provide a detailed record of the discourse. Field notes are taken while video-recording. The content of the field notes includes details regarding the general atmosphere of the classroom, teacher's and students' unique behaviour and utterances and their attitudes towards classroom activities. A semi-structured interview is conducted with the teacher before collecting classroom interaction data in order to get information about the teachers' professional training, their linguistic knowledge, their perception of the best EMI pedagogy, and their attitudes towards using multiple languages in the classrooms. Various informal interviews are undertaken with the teacher in order to better understand the observed lessons. A video-stimulated interview is conducted with the participating teacher. Before conducting the interviews, video-clips which reveal salient features of teachers' translanguaging practices are chosen by me as the stimulus. The teacher is asked to watch the selected video-clips and reflect on his use of translanguaging in particular EMI classroom micro-contexts. This allows the teacher to reflect on his own pedagogical practices and offers me a chance to verify certain things that are not clear from the classroom observations.

When analysing classroom video data, I look for translanguaging instances which involves going beyond different linguistic structures and systems (i.e., not only different languages and dialects but also styles, registers, and other variations in language use) and different modalities (e.g., switching between speaking and writing, or coordinating gestures, body movements, facial expressions, visual images). The identification of translanguaging instances in the data will be relied on the analysis of the interaction itself.

MCA analysis of the video data first involves adhering to the principle of "unmotivated" looking. This requires the researchers to ground the research focus based on the recordings of the interactions without referring to the external factors unacknowledged by the participants in order to develop an emic understanding of the classroom interaction. Line-by-line analysis is conducted to examine how talk is sequentially organised on a turn-by-turn basis, relating each utterance to what has been said before and what comes after (Kasper, 2009). After conducting line-by-line analysis, I analyse the ethnographic data so that it allows for the data to be triangulated and provides different interpretations of the roles of translanguaging practices in different classroom moments. In order to ensure that the MCA analyses are not affected by the ethnographic information gained from participants as well as my own perspective as a participant observer, any analytical claims regarding the classroom video data should be evidenced in the details of the interaction (Seedhouse, 2004).

The feasibility trial confirms that combining multimodal CA with an ethnographic approach as a method to analyse the classroom interaction is appropriate since CA allows me to identify examples of the teacher's translanguaging practices. I am able to triangulate my CA analysis with the ethnographic data in order to understand how and why translanguaging is constructed at that moment of the interaction. The classroom findings demonstrate that translanguaging enables the teacher to utilise various linguistic, multimodal, and spatial resources, and his sociocultural and pedagogical knowledge to achieve his pedagogical goals at particular moments in the lessons and create new meanings. In particular, I have found that playful talk as an EMI classroom micro-context can play a role in transforming the classroom momentarily into a translanguaging space which in turn allows teacher and students to perform a range of subversive acts and experiment a variety of voices to facilitate the meaning-making processes (Tai & Li, 2020a). Through these creative translanguaging practices, the teacher creates a translanguaging space which in turn facilitates expansion of students' communicative repertoires for learning content knowledge and constructing knowledge in the EMI classrooms.

The feasibility trial highlights the importance of the video-stimulated-recall interviews. I discover that conducting the video-stimulated-recall interview with the teacher allows me to understand the teacher's translanguaging practices as lived experience. The teacher also comments that the interview is a reflective process for him to make sense of his own pedagogical practices. I employ Interpretative Phenomenological Analysis (IPA) to analyse the video-stimulated-recall-interview data and it is shown as a useful method to explore how the EMI mathematics teacher makes sense of his translanguaging practices. The analysis involves a dual interpretation process called "double hermeneutic" which requires me to try to make sense of the teacher trying to make sense of his world (Smith, Flowers, & Larkin, 2013). By doing so, it enables me to take an "insider's perspective" (Conrad, 1987) in order to understand the teacher's personal experience. The findings reveal several superordinate themes (see Tai &Li, 2020a, 2020b, 2020c for the detailed analysis):

- Translanguaging as a means for bridging students' knowledge gap
- Translanguaging as a means for promoting students' responses
- The role of the teacher's prior life experience in shaping his translanguaging practices
- Translanguaging as a way for motivating student interest in the content subject
- Translanguaging as a way to bridge the social distance between the teacher and students

9.3 Concluding thoughts

In this feasibility trail, I have described some of the processes that I have gone through during my study and the issues that I have had to consider. I have shown that MCA can potentially be deployed to understand how teacher and students draw on various multilingual and multimodal resources to construct meanings in EMI classroom interactions. Moreover, I further emphasise the need to adopt an ethnographic approach since it can be used to support and expand the linguistic analysis (e.g., MCA). Collecting ethnographic data can also allow researchers to understand how classroom participants bring in their funds of knowledge to the fore-front, including their linguistic knowledge and cultural and life experi-ences, to construct their translanguaging practices for expressing their ideas and promoting content learning. Bringing the ethnographic data to bear offers unique insights into the "dynamics of social and cultural production" (Rampton et al., 2004) which a linguistic analysis alone may not always deliver. This chapter has sought to make the case for studying linguistic and ethnographic data together in order to produce detailed analysis of the construction of translanguaging practices in EMI classrooms.

This chapter also reinforces the need for researchers to have a clear understanding of the concept of translanguaging. A number of scholars narrowly define translanguaging as "fluid use of multiple languages" to maximise meaning potential. However, it is vital to reconsider whether using multiple named languages is sufficient enough to be considered as translanguaging. How does the interactional features differ from the term "codeswitching"? Leading proponents of translanguaging (e.g., Li, 2018) have clearly argued that translanguaging does not only involve using mul-tiple "named" languages. Hence, it is important for researchers to have a better understanding of the conceptualisation of translanguaging as a theory of language.

The concept of translanguaging invites researchers to reconceptualise language from the traditional notion of speech and writing to a multilingual, multimodal, multisensory, and multi-semiotic meaning-making resources. Employing LE as a methodological framework enables researchers to cap-ture the dynamic, flexible, and momentary actions that multilinguals do. By doing so, it enables researchers and EMI teachers to understand how translanguaging can potentially be used as a pedagogical tool to develop students' communicative repertoire for knowledge construction, alleviate the language barriers to learning academic concepts, and counteract stu-dents' linguistic insecurity in the EMI classrooms.

References

Antaki, C. (2012). What actions mean, to whom, and when. *Discourse Studies*, *14*, 493–498.

Conrad, P. (1987). The experience of illness: Recent and new directions. *Research in the Sociology of Health Care*, *6*, 1–31.

Copland, F. (2011). Negotiating face in feedback conferences: A linguistic ethno-graphic Analysis. *Journal of Pragmatics*, *43*, 3832–3843.

Copland, F., & Creese, A. (2015). *Linguistic ethnography: Collecting, analysing and presenting data*. Los Angeles: Sage.

Coyle, D., Hood, P., & Marsh, D. (2010). *CLIL: Content and language integrated learning*. Cambridge: Cambridge University Press.

Creese, A., & Blackledge, A. (2010). Translanguaging in the bilingual classroom: A pedagogy for learning and teaching. *Modern Language Journal, 94*, 103–115.

Duarte, J. (2019). Translanguaging in mainstream education: A sociocultural approach. *International Journal of Bilingual Education and Bilingualism, 22*(2), 1–15.

Firth, A., & Wagner, J. (1997). On discourse, communication, and (some) fundamental concepts in SLA research. *Modern Language Journal, 81*, 285–300.

Ford, C. (2012). Clarity in applied and interdisciplinary conversation analysis. *Discourse Studies, 14*, 507–513.

García, O. (2009). *Bilingual education in the 21st century: A global perspective*. Malden, MA: Wiley-Blackwell.

Gierlinger, E. (2015). 'You can speak German, sir': On the Complexity of Teachers' L1 Use in CLIL. *Language and Education, 29*, 347–368.

Hornberger, N. H., & Link, H. (2012). Translanguaging in today's classrooms: A biliteracy lens. *Theory into Practice, 51*, 239–247.

Jefferson, G. (2004). Glossary of transcript symbols with an introduction. In G. Lerner (Ed.), *Conversation analysis: Studies from the first generation* (pp. 14–31). Philadelphia: John Benjamins.

Kasper, G. (2009). Locating cognition in second language interaction and learning: Inside the skull or in public view? *International Journal of Applied Linguistics in Language Teaching, 47*(1), 11–36.

Li, W. (2011). Moment analysis and translanguaging space: Discursive construction of identities by multilingual Chinese youth in Britain. *Journal of Pragmatics, 43*, 1222–1235.

Li, W. (2014). Translanguaging knowledge and identity in complementary classrooms for multilingual minority ethnic children. *Classroom Discourse, 5*, 158–175.

Li, W. (2018). Translanguaging as a practical theory of language. *Applied Linguistics, 39*, 9–30.

Lin, A. M. Y., & He, P. (2017). Translanguaging as dynamic activity flows in CLIL classrooms. *Journal of Language, Identity and Education, 16*, 228–244.

Lin, A. M. Y., & Lo, Y. Y. (2017). Trans/languaging and the triadic dialogue in content and language integrated learning (CLIL) classrooms. *Language and Education, 31*, 26–45.

Lin, A. M. Y., & Wu, Y. (2015). "May I speak Cantonese?" e Co-constructing a scientific proof in an EFL junior secondary science classroom. *International Journal of Bilingual Education and Bilingualism, 18*(3), 289–305.

Lo, Y. Y. (2015). How much L1 is too much? – Teachers' language use in response to students' abilities and classroom interaction in CLIL. *International Journal of Bilingual Education and Bilingualism, 18*, 270–288.

Macaro, E. (2018). *English medium instruction*. Oxford: Oxford University Press.

Markee, N., & Kasper, G. (2004). Classroom talks: An introduction. *Modern Language Journal, 88*, 491–500.

Matsumoto, Y. (2018). Functions of laughter in English-as-a-lingua-franca classroom interactions: A multimodal ensemble of verbal and nonverbal interactional resources at miscommunication moments. *Journal of English as a Lingua Franca, 7*, 229–260.

Mazak, C., & Herbas-Donoso, C. (2015). Translanguaging practices at a bilingual university: A case study of a science classroom. *International Journal of Bilingual Education and Bilingualism, 18*, 698–714.

Mazak, C. M., & Carroll, K. S. (Eds.). (2016). *Translanguaging in higher education: Beyond monolingual ideologies*. Bristol: Multilingual Matters.

McCarthy, M. (1991). *Discourse analysis for language teachers*. Cambridge: Cambridge University Press.

Mondada, L. (2019). Contemporary issues in conversation analysis: Embodiment and materiality, multimodality and multisenoriality in social interaction. *Journal of Pragmatics, 145*, 47–62.

Moore, E. (2014). Constructing content and language knowledge in plurilingual student teamwork: Situated and longitudinal perspectives. *International Journal of Bilingual Education and Bilingualism, 17*(5), 586–609.

Moore, E., & Vallejo, C. (2018). Practices of conformity and transgression in an out-of-school reading programme for 'at risk' children. *Linguistics and Education, 43*, 25–38.

Nikula, T., & Moore, P. (2019). Exploring translanguaging in CLIL. *International Journal of Bilingual Education and Bilingualism, 22*(2), 1–12.

Pomerantz, A. (2012). Do participants' reports enhance conversation analytic claims? Explanation of one sort or another. *Discourse Studies, 14*, 499–505.

Potter, J. (1996). Discourse analysis and constructionist approaches: Theoretical background. In J. T. E. Richards (Ed.), *Handbook of qualitative research methods for psychology and the social sciences* (pp. 125–140). Leicester: British Psychological Society.

Probyn, M. (2019). Pedagogical translanguaging and the construction of science knowledge in a multilingual South African classroom: Challenging monoglossic/post-colonial orthodoxies. *Classroom Discourse, 10*, 216–236.

Psathas, G. (1995). *Conversation analysis: The study of talk-in-interaction*. London: Sage.

Rampton, B. (2006). *Language in late modernity: Interaction in an urban school*. Cambridge: Cambridge University Press.

Rampton, B. (2007). Linguistic ethnography, interactional sociolinguistics, and the study of identities. *Working Papers in Urban Language & Literacies*, 1–14.

Rampton, B., Tusting, K., Maybin, J., Barwell, R., Creese, A., & Lytra, V. (2004). *UK linguistic ethnography: A discussion paper*. Retrieved from www.lancaster.ac.uk/fss/organisations/ lingethn/documents/discussion_paper_jan_05.pdf.

Seedhouse, P. (2004). *The interactional architecture of the language classroom: A conversation analysis perspective*. London: Blackwell.

Smith, J. A., Flowers, P., & Larkin, M. (2013). *Interpretative phenomenological analysis: Theory, method, and research*. Los Angeles, CA: Sage.

Tai, K. W. H., & Brandt, A. (2018). Creating an imaginary context: Teacher's use of embodied enactments in addressing a learner's initiatives in a beginner-level adult ESOL classroom. *Classroom Discourse, 9*, 244–266.

Tai, K. W. H., & Khabbazbashi, N. (2019a). Vocabulary explanations in beginning-level adult ESOL classroom interactions: A conversation analysis perspective. *Linguistics and Education, 52*, 61–77.

Tai, K. W. H., & Khabbazbashi, N. (2019b). The mediation and organisation of gestures in vocabulary instructions: A microgenetic analysis of interactions in a beginning-level adult ESOL classroom. *Language and Education, 33*, 445–468.

Tai, K. W. H., & Li, W. (2020a). Constructing playful talk through translanguaging in the English medium instruction mathematics classrooms. *Applied Linguistics*, Epub ahead of print.

Tai, K. W. H., & Li, W. (2020b). Bringing the outside in: Connecting students' out-of-school knowledge and experience through translanguaging in Hong Kong EMI classes. *System, 95*, 1–32.

Tai, K. W. H., & Li, W. (2020c). Co-learning in Hong Kong English medium instruction mathematics secondary classrooms: A translanguaging perspective. *Language and Education*, Epub ahead of Print.

ten Have, P. (2001). Applied conversation analysis. In A. McHoul & M. Rapley (Eds.), *How to analyse talk in institutional settings: A casebook of methods* (pp. 3–11). London: Continuum.

Walsh, S. (2011). *Exploring classroom discourse: Language in action.* London: Routledge.

Wang, D. (2019). Translanguaging in Chinese foreign language classrooms: Students and teachers' attitudes and practices. *International Journal of Bilingual Education and Bilingualism, 22*, 138–149.

Wetherell, M. (2007). A step too far: Discursive psychology, linguistic ethnography and questions of identity. *Journal of Sociolinguistics, 11*(5), 662–681.

Williams, C. (1994). An evaluation of teaching and learning methods in the context of bilingual secondary education (PhD thesis). University of Wales, Bangor.

Index

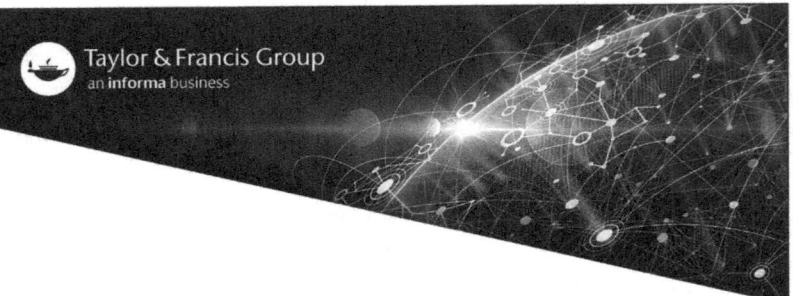